The Successful New CEO

The Successful New CEO

The Core Leadership Principles
That Will Guide Your First Year

Christian Muntean

BUSINESS EXPERT PRESS

Leader in applied, concise business books

The Successful New CEO: The Core Leadership Principles That Will Guide Your First Year

Copyright © Business Expert Press, LLC, 2020.

Cover image licensed by Ingram Image, StockPhotoSecrets.com

Cover and interior design by Exeter Premedia Services Private Ltd., Chennai, India

First published in 2020 by
Business Expert Press, LLC
222 East 46th Street, New York, NY 10017
www.businessexpertpress.com

ISBN-13: 978-1-95253-808-7 (paperback)
ISBN-13: 978-1-95253-809-4 (e-book)

Business Expert Press Human Resource Management and Organizational Behavior Collection

Collection ISSN: 1946-5637 (print)
Collection ISSN: 1946-5645 (electronic)

First edition: 2020

10 9 8 7 6 5 4 3 2 1

Printed in the United States of America.

Abstract

I've coached hundreds of leaders across many industries. Many of whom were new CEOs. Sometimes they use other titles: President, Managing Partner, General Manager, Executive Director, Principal, or something more creative. But they were all at the pointy part of the organizational pyramid.

This book is birthed from that experience. While every CEO and organization is unique, there are many common experiences, situations, and decisions. This book shines a light on those and illustrates the key principles that will guide a CEO through them.

The Successful New CEO is divided into four parts:

Becoming an Executive: Leaders can only lead out of who they are. How do you become the kind of person who successfully and gracefully inhabits this role?

Seven Essential Executive Skills: The skills that earned you the role may not be what you need in that role. What are the key leadership skills that become even more important at the executive level?

Leading Your Leadership Team: More than likely, you'll be leading other leaders. How do you lead a confident, effective leader? How do you build a team out of leaders?

First Things: Where do you start? How do you quickly build credibility and engagement? What is too fast or too slow?

The goal of the book is to help you to quickly gain the confidence of your team, successfully address the issues you will discover, score early wins, and set the course for a fruitful future.

Keywords

New executive; new leader; new CEO; First 90 days; First 100 days; First year; Biggest mistakes; How to be a CEO

Contents

Acknowledgments

I would like to acknowledge Brian Green who has been a mentor to me. I have often thought, "What would Brian do?" when facing a tough leadership situation.

I would also like to also acknowledge my wife, Marta. Your consistent support and encouragement is the platform that holds me up.

Additionally, I would like to acknowledge Wendy Hall, who has helped me edit my books. You take the pain out of the editing process, and that is much appreciated.

Finally, I acknowledge Jesus Christ. Without your example, servant leadership would always be beyond me.

Foreword

It was January, and I had arrived! No, not because it was the new year but I was finally the CEO of a scrappy company that I had been working in and developing for the last five years.

With all of the work, long nights, and personal growth I had put in to get to that point, I expected to wake up the next morning with a sense of vision, clarity, and purpose that was unmatched. The mantle had fallen, and it would be a magical moment! What I woke up to instead is a very clear sense that yesterday I knew what I was doing and how to be productive, and now I had no idea what I was doing. How could this be? I had spent all of that time growing as a leader, growing myself, the company, and others and yet I felt lost. I knew the company, knew the reason we existed, and somehow when the buck stopped with me and there was nowhere to hide; it was just different. As prepared as I was, I was not prepared for the mirage of complexity, and the feeling that I always needed to be out in front of everything always. I was the CEO after all! Oh, did I mention the competing priorities and the never-ending demands on my time? What about having fear, stress, and anxiety always knocking at my door? Sounds familiar? Sounds fun?

Welcome to your first year as a CEO.

The time, attention, and growth that goes into being able to "arrive" at the CEO seat is tremendous. That day that finally comes, and you get to put an executive title next to your name, but then you realize you are prepared for that day, and not the next. You just found yourself at the starting line. Even with the level of diligence that no doubt you have to even be a part of the executive conversation, you now find yourself on a new path full of opportunities and challenges that you are not prepared for.

The first-year CEO is like the first year of marriage: So much time, planning, and preparing for the day you will get to say "I do." You then wake up the next day in an entirely new reality and realize that you either spent very little time knowing how to be a great partner and spouse, or you prepared the best you can and you now know that nothing truly prepares you until you find yourself there.

Fast forward to today, 12 years later I am the president and chairman of the board for that company, having raised up a truly fantastic CEO to replace myself. I now have the privilege of being the CEO of another fast-growing company.

My story of being a first-year CEO, as well as the story of my successor (who you will hear from next), has something special that many people don't: Christian Muntean.

I have known Christian now for over two decades and have experienced firsthand what he has to offer. Not only have I benefited, but I have also watched several other executives, corporations, non-profits, and even countries benefit from his clear, simple, actionable leadership coaching and writing. I used the principles in this book to guide me and my successor through the rough waters of leading ourselves first so we didn't burn out, building our executive skill set so that we could get results, and unlock the potential in others around us so that our leadership was able to multiply.

If you choose to apply and master the concepts in this book, you will find yourself equipped and confident to tackle the journey ahead. Use this book as a manual for growth, and you will find yourself thriving as a highly accountable, highly influential, and growing-from-the-core-out executive.

I am truly excited for you and the impact you can make in the CEO seat. Are you up to the challenge? If you want to know if it is worth it, I can clearly and emphatically say yes! The job will push and stretch you beyond what you can imagine, and the person you will become if you choose will be someone you are very proud of.

I and all those that have gone before you are rooting for you!

Reed Moore
President and Chairman
RMG Real Estate Network

My first memory of Christian was listening to him at a company retreat. He was leading our team through exercises to better our conflict resolution skills. At the time I didn't even know what that meant. Only a few hours into the retreat controversial ideas, concerns, and thoughts were all being aired openly and people were a bit heated. I won't lie; I was a little nervous. After the initial shock of watching my colleagues and boss having it out I realized that we were slowly becoming closer as the event went on. The honesty and realness of the conversations were giving us a connection or bond we hadn't experienced yet. I walked away wanting to learn more from him.

Fast forward a few years and I am the CEO of that very same company. Overnight I realized that how I lead within the team up until that point got me to where I was and absolutely wasn't going to cut it moving forward. I needed direction, coaching, and a better skillset to lead a company that was growing everyday. It wasn't long before I found myself sitting across from Christian Muntean with the same feeling I remember from years prior; I don't know what I don't know.

Christian and the principles in his book were paramount in helping me navigate the complexities of the CEO role, growing the culture and getting results as a company. Through his guidance, I quickly realized that creativity without a foundation of models and proven principles would lead to a short-lived success. He helped me lay the foundation for a company that could do year over year growth without jeopardizing the culture that got it this far. I learned to collaborate in a way that brought greater strength to the company, truly mine for disagreement and unleash the brilliance in the people I lead. Without a doubt I owe a tremendous amount to Christian and what he is about to teach you in *First Year CEO*.

Annie Bjerkestrand
CEO
RMG Real Estate Network

Introduction

I am fascinated with leadership and the dynamics that surround it. Additionally, I am fascinated by my clients, their varied visions and stories, and the effort they put into building and bringing value.

As an executive coach and consultant, I often work with new CEOs or an equivalent position. Because of the massive demographic shift of Baby Boomers moving out of the workplace, there may be more new CEOs arriving into their positions than ever before.

If this is you: You may be succeeding a long-time leader at an established company. You might be the first CEO ever hired at a fast-growth company. You might be a president or managing partner, who, with your partners, is trying to understand the difference between ownership and organizational leadership.

Whatever the case, you are likely very smart, committed, and capable. You are probably experienced as a leader and have a track record of success.

You have also discovered, or will soon, that being in the executive seat is often different than expected.

That is common. The CEO role, the pointy part of the pyramid, is a unique position.

Some new CEOs discover they have far less authority than they expected. Or that they have insufficient direction, with unclear or conflicting expectations from ownership or the board. Or they are inheriting the responsibility for challenges they did not create.

If hired from within, the transition from *peer* to *superior* is often confusing and complicated. These CEOs may be dealing with undealt issues from the previous regime. Or from their own history. There may be changes in the nature of relationships and friendships.

Much of my work is around helping new executives get up to speed quickly and succeed. That is why I wrote this book. In it I address the topics and issues that most commonly emerge in my work with new CEOs.

Initially, it was intended to be a short e-book compiled from previous articles and essays that I've written. However, as I outlined the key topics and looked at what I had already written, I realized a complete book made more sense. While I've worked to smooth it out and fill in gaps and reduce repetition, the reader may still notice a flow and cadence that reflects the origins of the book.

The book is organized into four sections:

Section I: Becoming the CEO focuses on the *person* of the leader. There is no single *CEO type*. However, you can only lead out of who you are. This section focuses on who you need to be, or become, to succeed as a CEO.

Section II: Seven Executive Skills focuses on the key skills you need as a CEO. The reader will notice that these are all soft skills. A CEO often comes to their position because of a strong technical or professional background. But, more than anything, you to be an effective leader of people. This will clarify the essential executive skills that you need for success.

Section III: Leading Your Leadership Team helps orient you to the bulk of your new role: leading your leadership team. Your effectiveness as a CEO is directly associated with your ability to grow and lead other leaders. This section explores how to identify new senior leaders and work with them effectively.

Section IV: First Things focuses on what you should do first. Everyone's experience stepping into the CEO role for the first time is a little different. The circumstances surrounding each leadership transition are unique. But, there are common dynamics that occur for most executives. This section helps prepare you for those.

I wrote these sections and chapters with the goal of allowing you to choose whether you read the whole book from back to front or skip around and choose the topic you need.

My hope is that this book will help you earn quick, meaningful wins, avoid (or rapidly correct) the common errors many new CEOs make, and build a foundation that will allow many years of continued growth and success.

Take good care.

Christian Muntean

PART I

Becoming an Executive

CHAPTER 1

You, the Right Person in the Right Place

Leadership development is personal development.
Your growth as a leader follows your growth as a person.

Why Would Anyone Follow You?

When I teach leadership, I often conduct the following exercise with a group. I ask, "What is one word that describes a leader?" I have conducted this exercise in multiple cultures and countries. The answers are always similar:

- *Caring*
- *Takes charge*
- *Direction*
- *Mentor*
- *Helps*
- *Vision*
- *Solves problems*

And so on.

Next, I ask, "How many of these words seem positive? Neutral? Negative?" In nearly all cases, the words are either positive or neutral.

Then, I ask, "Have you ever had a leader who did not demonstrate these words?" The room will always start to laugh, shift in their seats, or begin to make comments. Everyone has experienced a leader who not only did not demonstrate the positive words but also lived out negative ones.

My observation: At a gut level, people viscerally want leaders who can be trusted and relied on to look out for the interests of others.

Then, I ask, "How many of you consistently live out this list of words in your leadership role?"

The room always gets pretty quiet.

What People Want from Leaders

At the most basic level, at the level of motivation and commitment, people want three things from their leaders:

- They want a leader who has a clear sense of direction or purpose.
- They want a leader who is competent.
- They want a leader who cares about them.

Offer these three things and leadership is not difficult. So...why is leadership so difficult?

Common, Shaky Foundations for Leadership

I have recently worked with the boards of two different corporations. In both cases, leadership was defined as "I have (or control) a majority of the votes."

Many leaders feel like their ability to lead is based on their title or position. Or perhaps in their experience, or technical expertise, or that they have *power*. But none of these things actually creates *leadership*. At least, not the kind of leadership that has willing followers. Title, position, and resources all may be influential. But people are not following *you*. They are following the title, the position, or the resources. Power is influential, but it is coercive and temporary. People will only move as far as they are pushed or pulled. People will only follow as long as you retain the power to push or pull. Enormous energy and effort are required to maintain this.

In the case of the boards aforementioned, this power-based approach to leadership has weakened both companies. It has led to factions. It has squelched innovation and drive on the part of the less powerful. It generates resentment. It diverts energy toward boardroom intrigues and away from actually building the business.

Interestingly, the directors of both boards regularly complain that they do not have the time to do the work of leadership. But, that does not prevent them from putting enormous time into all the problems and drama stemming from poor leadership.

Leadership Made Easy

It takes something different to be a person who is willingly followed by others. To be a person who is a leader. This kind of person will be followed and have influence regardless of their title, position, or resources. They may not even have any direct power.

We live in a time where many societies are experiencing high levels of anxiety. Levels of distrust and cynicism regarding positions of authority and the people who fill them are high. The high speed of change requires full attention and rapid responses to opportunities and challenges. Time and attention spent anywhere else is the leadership equivalent of texting while driving.

Leadership is critically necessary. But, people are increasingly wary of the people called *leaders*.

The Path to Legitimate Power and Greatness

To be successful over the long term requires an uncommon, but powerfully effective approach.

The 1960s were another season of unrest, anxiety, and change—as well as a great time of opportunity. Perhaps similar to now. At that time, a man named Robert Greenleaf was the director of management at AT&T. He noticed the dynamics I described and began to wrestle with how to train and equip leaders to lead in a way that others would willingly follow.

His philosophy can largely be summed up in the following quote: "The servant-leader is servant first…it begins with a natural feeling that one wants to serve, to serve *first*, as opposed to wanting power, influence, fame, or wealth."[1] This does not mean that a leader has no drive or ambition. To the contrary, the best leaders usually have enormous drive and ambition. What it does mean is that the nature of this ambition is different.

A contemporary researcher, Jim Collins, discovered the same dynamic and phrased it as such:

> We found that for leaders to make something great, their ambition has to be for the greatness of the work and the company, rather than for themselves.
>
> Smart people instinctively understand the dangers of entrusting our future to self-serving leaders who use our institutions, whether in the corporate or social sectors, to advance their own interests (Collins 2001).[2]

Robert Greenleaf called his model of leadership a *servant-leader*. Jim Collins calls his a *Level 5 Leader*. Either way, they both identified that it is a different kind of leader, driven by a different set of motivations, who generates *greatness*.

How Do You Start?

It is actually pretty simple.

The most effective and influential leaders use this question to calibrate how they lead:

What Will Bring the Greatest Value or Purpose to Those Who Follow Me?

Not sure if you agree? Think about the leaders you most respect. What is it that you respect about them? To what degree did they bring value or purpose to those they led?

---

[1] Greenleaf, R.K. 2002. *Servant Leadership: A Journey into the Nature of Legitimate Power and Greatness*. Paulist Press.

[2] Collins, Jim. 2001. *Good to Great: Why Some Companies Make the Leap ... and Others Don't*. Harper Business.

It's been my experience that most people will say that they leaders they most respect are also the leaders who somehow brought great value or connected them to a greater purpose.

Now…what can you do to bring the greatest value to those around you? If leadership is a tool you can use to accomplish this, you are on the right track.

Regardless of the kind of work you are in or where you lead, answer that question. As you grow in your ability to bring that value or accomplish that purpose, people will automatically follow you. You will not have to work at it.

> *What about those you lead now? What seems to be most important to them? What is onething you can do to bring value or a sense of purpose to those you lead?*

How to Know if a CEO Position Is Right for You

Executive opportunities can be seductive.

If you have never held an executive position before—the opportunity, the power, the office, the salary—it can be heady stuff. Even at small organizations.

If you are an experienced executive, you know how difficult it can be to consider any other role after being an executive.

However, not all executive opportunities are created equal. Some are fantastic opportunities, with healthy organizations and great teams. Others are like being recruited to be captain of a toxic, funky, sinking ship. But, not everyone can tell those opportunities apart.

On top of this, every healthy leader has a high sense of self-efficacy. You believe you can make a difference. You believe you can influence and change things. If you do not believe that, you should not be in a leadership role.

The downside? Sometimes, leaders overestimate their abilities or underestimate the challenges. Sometimes, they just are not given all the information.

Most often, because they did not ask.

Perhaps, you are a candidate for the position. But, that organization should also be a candidate for your skills, time, and energy. Interview them as well.

Perhaps, you have already accepted the position. As CEO, you accept responsibility for outcomes. But, ideal outcomes cannot be achieved or sustained when there are obvious issues within the organization, board, or ownership.

While you cannot control the external environment, you should be a shaper of your internal environment. It is an important part of leadership to ensure the conditions you need to generate success. Otherwise, *you can and should expect* to be blamed for situations others have created.

Here is a secret that most boards, owners, or outgoing CEOs do not want you to know: They usually are not sure what they should look for in an executive. Often, their decision-making comes down to one of the four things:

- **A candidate who is exactly like the person being replaced**. This is change-resistant and uncreative. It indicates a back-ward-looking approach. While this happens in very conservative or traditional organizations, it is also common in organizations led by dynamic, entrepreneurial leaders. It is common for very strong and successful leaders to want to replicate themselves.
- **A candidate who is absolutely not like the previous (prob-lem) person**. This is reactive and provides no direction or sense of why you are a fit or what you should accomplish.
- **They just like a candidate**. Skills or capacity can be irrele-vant. This is a subjective and emotional decision. It leaves you vulnerable to a change in opinions or the political wind.
- **Qualities unrelated to executive leadership**. Many exec-utives achieve their position because they were good at something else. Or they were around the longest. Or they demonstrated loyalty over the years. All of which can be posi-tive things. None of which directly supports executive success. Boards and owners are frequently more reactive than strate-gic. More often than you might imagine, they will make the choice that requires the least amount of effort on their part.

Because boards or owners often do not know what they are looking for or how to go about the process, it best serves everyone if you help them out. These questions are equally valid if you are an internal or external candidate for the position.

Twelve Questions You Should Ask

1. What Are the Critical Priorities and Goals of the Board/Owners?

As an executive, you still work for and report to someone. Often, several people. Make sure you know what is most important to them.

This should include strategic or business priorities as well as organizational culture and values. They may not have a specific strategy in mind, but they should know their very high-level priorities. If they do not, they should at least be willing to give them serious consideration.

2. What Are the Major Opportunities and Challenges Facing the Organization?

Look for their awareness of the environment they are operating in and their ability to answer this question. Ideally, they are a strong source of accurate and useful information.

Additionally, look for their ability to answer this question from both internal and external perspectives. In other words, they should be aware of the major operational opportunities or challenges as well as those coming from the environment.

There are no perfect organizations or situations. A great board or owner knows this, is looking for someone to partner with, and will be appropriately transparent with you.

3. What Has Worked or Not Worked in the Past Relationship between the Board or Owner and the Previous CEO? What Would They Like to Change or Keep?

Most of the time, you will only be offered this information if you are being hired after a negative experience with someone. But, it is not uncommon to be next in line to an emotionally loaded situation, which you may know nothing about.

However, if you are following a well-liked and trusted CEO, they likely have developed an informal set of practices and habits in the relationship. Unless you ask about them, they are not likely to think to tell you. You do not want to run into a situation of getting hit sideways with uncommunicated expectations.

4. Are There Any Legal, Health and Safety, or Ethical Issues or Practices within the Company?

With this question, you are looking for several things:

First, it is the face-value answers. You will want to know what you are walking into, especially because you will likely be held responsible for it.

Second, are they willing to be open and honest with you? Walk away immediately if they are not.

Third, look for patterns over time. Does this organization show a pattern of operating unethically? Have they tolerated unsafe work practices? Do they plan? Do they follow through on their plans? For how long have these patterns existed? Why?

5. What Is Their Financial Position? What Is Their Financial Philosophy?

This is very similar to the previous question. Make sure you know and can handle whatever you are stepping into.

You also want to make sure that you can get the quality of information you need when you need it. It is not uncommon in small and medium businesses for financial reporting to be, let us call it: thin. Even large organizations that are not publicly held can have surprisingly poor financial management or reporting. Do not make assumptions about financial health or the quality of reporting. Look for yourself.

Additionally, you want to gain a sense of their risk tolerance, their views on growth, diversification, savings, and caring for employees and shareholders. Even if the organization is a nonprofit or government agency, not a business, it needs to be healthy financially. You will want to know what *financially healthy* looks like to those in charge.

I once volunteered time with a nonprofit whose board believed that financially healthy meant it operated at exactly its cost. Literally, zero reserves.

Which worked fine until it stopped working. This was a board comprised primarily of university professors. They were smart people. But, do not make assumptions about what people know. Especially about finances.

6. What Will Be Your Scope of Decision-Making Authority?

This may be an evolving conversation, but you should always know where you are at any given point of time.

- What decisions are off the table?
- What decisions require a consult with the board or owners?
- Is anyone else involved in the decision-making? (Some owners or boards rely heavily on the input of a spouse, friend, trusted employee, or external advisor.)
- Which decisions are fully yours to make?

7. What Control Will You Have Over Personnel Decisions (Including Others in Management)?

This is very similar to the previous question. What is unique here is that it is common to hear, "You are free to make whatever choices seem right," and then discover that there are protected people, roles, or rights reserved by owners or board members to drop in new hires or promotions of their choosing.

Best practices are that a CEO has a free hand with personnel decisions—to create the best possible team to accomplish the goals. The reality is that most of the time, there are conditions or exceptions to this. If they exist, make sure you know them, are comfortable with them, and can succeed in that context.

8. What Does Turnover Look Like Here?

High turnover is usually an immediate warning signal. Management will nearly always blame it on compensation. But, it is typically tied to job satisfaction, a sense of meaningful and challenging work, feeling appreciated or respected, or workplace relationships.

If unhealthy levels of turnover exist, you would be wise to suspect there is a problem. Ensure that you have a free hand to correct it.

On the other hand, extremely low turnover can *sometimes* represent another problem. In many ways, longevity and loyalty are assets. However, it is worth exploring the following:

- Are low performers typically retained and tolerated?
- Are there old-timer cliques?
- Will they shift loyalty to a new CEO?
- Are they open to changes?

9. How Does the Leadership or Management Team Relate to Each Other?

Are you walking into silos, turfs, and conflict? Are you walking into camaraderie and mutual support? Are they (unhealthily) competitive with each other or collaborative? What are their expectations in terms of being led?

You will want to know this in advance and determine if it is an environment you can excel in.

10. How Will Your Performance Be Measured?

You will be assessed. There is a high chance that the assessment will be more informal than formal. This is not the best practice, but it is how it usually works.

Because they likely will not have a formal assessment process, make sure you know, and keep current on, their expectations for your performance. Make sure they are specific, make sense to you, and are achievable.

If you can get them in writing, do so. If they do not provide them, send an e-mail saying something to the effect of, "I understand that you want A, B, C accomplishments, in X time frame, measured by Y and Z."

This provides that written record of their expectations and an opportunity for clarification early on, if needed.

11. Will They Provide You with Support for Personal/Professional Development?

As an executive, you need to continue to grow. You need to be exposed to new thinking. Executives do not have to be lonely, but you are no longer a peer with other in your organization. You will need peers and people who will be honest with you.

You benefit from someone outside your organization to bounce ideas off of or confide in. This can look like training, executive peer groups, mentors, or coaching. A board or owner who does not understand or value this kind of investment is severely limiting your ability to perform and improve.

12. Can You Talk to Employees Now?

Talk to those you will lead at various levels, roles, and locations. If you can, *shop* the workplace. When this is not possible, interview people. Visit the locations. Gain a sense of these things:

- Do employees seem happy at work?
- Are they doing their jobs well?
- Do they seem stressed? Why?
- What does the workplace environment look like—does it show signs of pride and care?
- Is there respectfulness toward each other and customers?

You may also see things with a troubleshooting eye. Noticing what could or should be changed. However, primarily look for strengths and assets. What makes people proud, what motivates them, what gets them up in the morning? Do not be philosophical about this. Get real answers. They will matter.

Here Is What Will Happen

An *ideal* board or owner will likely not expect most of these questions. They may not even be prepared with answers to all of them. But, they *will be* glad you asked them and work with you to get answers. Their respect for you will increase, as will their confidence.

You are asking the right questions.

They will see you as a partner to achieve their goals. They will work to build a strong relationship with you.

A *nonideal* board or owner will become defensive, minimize the importance of the information, or hide and distort information.

Let them self-select themselves *out* of the skills you have to offer. There are plenty of other, better opportunities. Do not waste your skills and energy for the wrong organization.

CHAPTER 2

Becoming an Executive

Becoming a leader is synonymous with becoming yourself. It is precisely that simple and it is also that difficult.

—Warren Bennis

How to Quickly Build a Magnetic Executive Presence

Two people walked onto the stage.

She walked in confidently and gave a warm smile to the audience. Her posture was straight and looked relaxed. Her humor was soft. She seemed like someone you would like to know.

As she spoke, she was direct and clear. I could see the direction she was describing. Without thinking about it, I found myself just believing that what she described was possible.

He followed her presentation. I knew him. He is a great guy. Solid character. Lots of management experience. He walked in with his head down. He was dressed in the casual, middle-aged teen look. He was humorous. Self-deprecating. People liked that.

They liked him. It took him a while to get to his point through the humor. To describe his vision. When he did, it was packed with qualifiers. In what was likely an attempt to be humble, he kept minimizing the vision, the value it would bring, or if he could even make it happen. I found myself agreeing with his self-assessment.

At the end, it was clear that they were both nice, competent people. Only one seemed like someone I would trust in a senior leadership role.

Perhaps we are thinking of the same person.

Only one had executive presence.

One of the most important leadership qualities is nebulously called executive presence. It is a topic that is missing from business schools. Leadership programs rarely discuss it. Your mentor is unlikely to bring it up. It will not be found on a job description.

But, people are looking for it.

In most cases, it is a required trait. If you do not have it, you can expect to experience a limit in your advancement as a leader.

However, having an executive presence does not even mean you can lead. But, if you want to be effective at a senior level, especially as a CEO, you need it.

What Is Executive Presence?

It is executive presence—and no man or woman attains a top job, lands an extraordinary deal, or develops a significant following without this heady combination of confidence, poise, and authenticity that convinces the rest of us we're in the presence of someone who's the real deal.

—Sylvia Ann Hewlett

Executive presence is someone's ability to quickly cause others to trust in his or her ability to lead. It is a perception that "This person can do this. This person can get us where we need to go."

That is it.

It is others' perception of you. A perception you helped create. If you have it, it results in an increase in influence. Your voice is heard more quickly and regarded more highly. You are able to create buy-in, agreement, and partnerships more easily.

Something about you gives people confidence. They believe if they stick close to you, good things will happen. It is an enabling trait.

People will want to follow you. People will want to work with you.

What It Is Not

Executive presence is *not* actually leadership. It sure helps you lead. But, it is not leadership on its own. Fortunately, cultivating your ability to lead can help develop your executive presence.

The Eight Qualities of Executive Presence

Leaders with executive presence possess eight qualities. Having only one or two is helpful. But, all eight are necessary to really create executive presence.

Happily, all of these qualities can be developed or grown.

1. Inspire Vision

People follow, partner with, and invest in others whom they believe are going somewhere. Your ability to imagine and describe a future that is inspirational to others is critical.

It does not even have to be your vision or your imagination. You might articulate and champion the inspiring vision of the team or group that you lead. That works just as well.

Whether you create it or you articulate it, you have to be able to inspire vision in others.

2. Cultivate Credibility

Credibility is the currency of leadership. People must believe you can be trusted. This means two things:

- You do what you say you will do.
- You have integrity: You tell the truth and are consistent in your actions.

What you do and have done matters. If you have not been reliable in the past, have been inconsistent in regard to integrity, or have a reputation for relating poorly to people, it will work against you. You need to develop a new track record.

Executive presence depends on credibility.

3. Project Confidence

You must believe in yourself and your team. You need to regularly reinforce those beliefs.

If you are uncertain, others will also be uncertain. Uncertainty undermines unity, alignment, and commitment. Unfortunately, some leaders confuse *confidence* with brashness or arrogance.

Here are handy differentiators:

- *Unjustified* confidence looks like brashness or foolishness. It is an empty suit: The belief one's success or capacity but without any reason or validation for that belief.
- *Arrogance* is always about comparisons. "I'm better, smarter, worth more, or more successful than someone else."
- *Justified confidence* comes from a substantiated belief that you have value and can bring value to others. That you can do the job at hand. This is the confidence that you need.

All leaders are confronted by times of fear or uncertainty. It is a basic fact of leadership: You will face an unknown future. People want and need your confidence about that future. They want to trust that you will lead them well. It is a gift to offer that.

4. Become Articulate

Generally, effective leaders are also good communicators. When someone can communicate clearly, concisely, and with ease, many people assume they can lead.

You can see this in group dynamics. If someone is articulate (including being concise), the group will tend to orient themselves around that individual. Their ideas do not even have to be good. People are drawn to, and influenced by, others who can frame their thoughts clearly.

If this is a challenge for you, a couple of practices can help:

- Read content on the topics you talk about. Learn how others communicate on those topics.
- Journal regularly. This helps develop the discipline of getting what is in you—out.
- Write articles to practice framing concepts clearly.

- Participate in groups like Toastmasters to help you learn to communicate more easily.

Some do not find this to be natural or easy. However, anyone can improve as a communicator. If you want people to follow you, you will need to spend time practicing your ability to communicate well.

5. Focus on Priorities

Many people lack confidence in their ability to set priorities. Usually, this comes from being afraid they are making the wrong choice. Or being uncomfortable with saying *No*.

When they meet someone who is focused on priorities, they often view that person as more confident and a better leader.

Learning to practice priority setting—for yourself, for your team, your family, your organization—all helps you cultivate that personal clarity of purpose. Others are drawn to this.

One very simple way to do this is to make a daily practice of writing a list of all the things you want to accomplish that day. Decide which one thing is the most important. Then structure your day to complete that one thing before moving on to the next one thing.

You will get more done. (You will!) And, you will be seen by others as being more intentional and focused. Prioritized.

6. Self-Discipline

New Year's resolutions are almost a joke. So many people make them, and so few follow through on them. Self-discipline eludes most people, whether it relates to hitting the gym or emotional control.

One of the fastest ways someone can lose credibility is to be seen as someone not in control of their own impulses. This includes impulses of passion (any strong emotion) or easily getting bored or losing interest. People naturally respect the ability of others to control and direct themselves.

Personally, I find the disciplines of fitness and mindfulness to be two ways to practice self-discipline. Research also supports these two habits as having broad benefits. Cultivating your abilities in these areas does translate into your leadership and executive presence.

For fitness, this can be as simple as taking a daily five-minute walk. That is all that is needed to start cultivating personal discipline.

For mindfulness, sitting still, meditating, or contemplative prayer, for even just five minutes, has value.

7. Physical Presence

Years ago, I was a volunteer mediator at small claims court. The mediators would sit in the jury box while the litigants arrived. We would all wait for the judge to begin the show.

While waiting, I would try to guess who the defendants and plaintiffs were. It was common for defendants to show up dressed poorly. Plaintiffs would usually dress up. This probably was not the most neutral exercise I could be engaged in as a mediator, but it passed the time.

One day, a man showed up whose hair was a mess. He had not shaved, his suit was mismatched and did not fit. He wore hiking boots.

I was sure he was a defendant. It turned out he was the attorney for one of the plaintiffs. We later got to know each other. It turns out he is highly intelligent with a box full of degrees, licenses, and certifications. But he did not inspire confidence with his first impression.

I'm a big fan of dressing casually. The part of the world I live in takes pride in its casualness. As a new mediator, I always wore jeans to court. Tucking my shirt in was my way of dressing up.

However, following that experience, I hurried to the nicest store in town and asked them to dress me.

That experience caused me to realize that I only had seconds for people to form an impression of me and either give or withhold their trust. Their trust in me was one of the primary ingredients in my ability to help these parties achieve a satisfactory agreement with each other.

If changing how I dressed helped them trust me, I would do so. Two simple changes can help you a lot.

- **Dress well**. Wear clothes at or just a notch more formal than the people you lead. People will relate to you differently. Just putting a suit on leads to being treated with more respect in some circles. This does not mean you always wear suits. But, look put together. If I am working with very blue-collar or rural clients, I will be more casual. But, it is still a nice casual. And, it matters to them.

- **Practice good posture.** Learning to sit and walk with good posture directly impacts how people perceive you. Slouching is completely disconnected from whether or not you can lead a team out of a wet paper bag. But, that is not what people will think.

Executive presence is about the impression that you make on others. Your physical presence is one of the most immediate and strongest impressions you can make. Make sure it is working for you.

8. Demonstrate Appreciation

Dr. Bob Nelson is a *New York Times* best-selling author and expert in employee engagement. He has observed, "An employee's motivation is a direct result of the sum of interactions with his or her manager."

He goes on to describe how the demonstration of recognition or appreciation by leaders to employees are primary motivators of sustained high performance.

Some leaders have the belief that, "You are paid to do the right thing. You don't need recognition for that." There is logic to that statement. But, that logic does not help you lead or create an environment where people want to follow you.

People like, feel safe, with and are drawn toward others who show them appreciation. Without appreciation, they may grow resentful, apathetic, or struggle with their own sense of self-worth.

How you make others feel impacts how they feel about you.

Putting It Together

An actor, with no leadership interest or capacity at all, can play a convincing and inspirational leader. A leader with presence. Someone you might feel inclined to follow.

Executive presence is about creating a perception.

For you to maintain credibility, you need to support the perception with real leadership. Executive presence will only go so far on its own. However, if you combine a strong executive presence with effective leadership, the limits are yours to construct.

How to Manage Yourself So That You Can Lead Others

A drowning man may drown you as well.

When learning water rescue techniques, the first lessons are how to keep yourself safe. Do not become another victim. The next lessons are how to defend yourself from someone who is drowning. From the person you are trying to rescue.

When someone is drowning, they panic. The panic can be so extreme that they become frantic. This may lead to wild thrashing, trying to climb onto anything that appears to float, or grabbing onto a rescue swimmer in such a way that the rescuer can no longer swim.

The frantic behavior costs them their already limited energy. It also makes them a danger. They are not responsive to instructions or guidance. They are fighting for survival.

Their fight is often part of what ends up killing them.

Frantic Leaders Are Dangerous Leaders

Helping a leader learn to manage their priorities and time is usually the first and most common challenge I face with a new client.

New leaders, particularly those in senior or executive positions, are often surprised by the immensity and unending nature of their responsibilities. It is not uncommon that they feel overwhelmed. As if they are drowning.

The sense of overwhelm quickly gives room for fear. The fear of being pulled under by underperformance, mistakes, failure, or revealed inabilities is so acute that many leaders lose perspective.

This panic translates into frantic, thrashing work behaviors.

Make no mistake about it; they are working. Working very hard. In fact, they are probably working harder than they need to or should be.

But, they are not working effectively. Not only that, but they begin to grab onto others to save themselves. Even people who are trying to help.

By not being able to protect themselves, by not knowing how to identify or receive help, they become a danger to others.

These leaders might start overwhelming others with task dumps or unrealistic expectations. They might place an unjust responsibility on others, blaming them for their own challenges.

They are drowning and taking others with them.

How to Protect Yourself So You Can Lead Others

Many of the executives and leaders I coach do not manage themselves well. They are maxed out, not in control of their schedules and at the mercy of everyone else's sense of urgency. In fact, experienced leaders often confuse having learned how to tread water with actually making progress.

When attempting a *rescue swim* with a leader in this situation, their cry for help sounds like:

"I'm overwhelmed. I have too much to do. I can't rely on my staff. No one else can get this done. Help!"

Then, as I start to work with them, they will protest, "I'm too busy to learn how to be less busy!"

Thrashing about in the water is not swimming. It is usually the precedent to sinking. You can float just fine by learning to relax and focus.

Own Your Priorities

You are busy. Deadlines and problems may be crushing you. There are endless meetings and requests by others and issues that break up your attention. Chaos and distractions are part of the normal package for most leaders.

Here Is the Deal

If you cannot learn to swim in choppy waters, you will never be able to lead. You will only be able to focus on survival.

Here Is the Good News

You can learn to swim. You can learn to be an excellent, strong, and confident swimmer who effortlessly appears to slice through the waves.

How

You have to stop the thrashing behaviors that made you feel safe but are not serving you well. You need to start learning new behaviors.

These new behaviors take less effort. They *will* save you time, lower your blood pressure, and make you better looking. (Well…maybe.)

But, they are new. New behaviors feel uncomfortable and unfamiliar. These are undesirable feelings when already feeling overwhelmed. This is often interpreted as having to do *even more*. Most leaders then revert to thrashing around.

So, do not be shy about getting help. That is the smart choice.

Here is some of that help.

Focus: Clarify What You Are Trying to Accomplish

Stephen Covey famously wrote, "Begin with the end in mind." In other words, obtain crystal clarity on what is important to you and what you are trying to accomplish.

When I work with leaders, I find that many of them have very short *horizons*. In other words, when I ask them to look out and describe the future, they may only be able to see clearly a few weeks or possibly a few months out. Some can easily see out a year or many years. Unfortunately, many struggle to see or maintain sight of that more distant horizon due to all immediate demands.

Wherever you are, however far you can see—that is fine. Start there.

I always encourage people to look out as far as they can and then stand on their tiptoes. Try to see just a smidge further over their horizon.

Get focused on where you need to end up in a few weeks or months. If you can see further out, go for it. Keep it very simple. Very focused. It is so much better to have just two or three goals. It is best to have one.

You need to focus.

Yes, everything else also needs to get done. And, it will. Or, enough of it will. (*Everything* never needs to actually get done. It just appears that way.)

But first, you need to focus.

Tip

Write down your focus point for the future. Be as specific and detailed as you can. See it. Describe what it will look like, how you know you are making progress and how you will know you have achieved it.

Prioritize Your Priorities

Many leaders will take the time to identify their priorities. But they don't take the next obvious step of prioritizing their priorities. When you look at their calendar or how they spend their days—you see what was actually prioritized. And, too often, it wasn't what they said was a priority.

Take a look at what you have written above. What are the key steps that you need to take to accomplish your focus? Some people like to plan this out backward. Some people like to plan it out forward.

Do whatever works easiest for you.

Then, start breaking it down into smaller goals or tasks. Put those in your calendar. Make these times sacred.

To make some things a priority, you'll need to get good at saying, "No" to many other things.

Success is often less about what we say "Yes" to and more about what we are willing to say "No" to.

Tips

(a) Map out your priorities.
(b) Put the time to work on them in your calendar.
(c) Protect these appointments with yourself.

Force Multiply

In the military, a force multiplier is anything that helps amplify the effectiveness of other groups or tactics.

Leaders, when operating well, are force multipliers. Teams should operate at a higher level because of your leadership. People should grow. Capacity and performance should increase.

This requires a shift away from thinking, "How am I going to do it all?" to "What do I need to do to help them do it all?"

Many leaders get overwhelmed because they do not know how to leverage the resources around them. This is more difficult when all of your goals or steps are locked up inside of you. It is much easier to work with others when they also can see what needs to be done.

That is what makes the previous steps important.

Now, decide. All of your tasks or steps should be able to fit into the following table. Preserve your focus for the items that require your leadership. Everything else should be given to others or dropped all together.

	Can others can do it?	What I must do
Does it move us closer to our focus?	Delegate and Support	Prioritize and Protect
Does it distract or prevent movement towards our focus?	Avoid, delay, or discard	

When you choose to do something that someone else could do, you are saying *No* to work that only you can do.

That limits your ability to accomplish your focus. It also creates a backlog of all the work you feel like you need to get done. It creates that sense of overwhelm.

Let Others Help You

The *primary way* a leader lets others help is by helping them do more on their own.

Letting others help you includes entrusting tasks, responsibilities, and authority to others. It also includes shifting your role from one of being a doer to one of being a mentor, a teacher, a cheerleader, a coach, a focused provider.

I recently spoke with a leader who was new in her senior leadership role. She is very smart and competent. She told me that she struggled with feeling like she was not working when she mentored, coached, or trained her staff.

Her staff told me that she works too much, that she does not give them enough to do. That she should let go of some of her responsibilities.

Clearly, there is a mismatch in perspectives. I am working to help her reframe what *work* looks like.

It goes back to shifting your question, as I mentioned earlier. Away from, "How am I going to do it all?" to "What do I need to do to help them do it all?"

A *second way* of letting others help you is to make sure that you are building relationships with those who strengthen you. This includes people like mentors (this includes both peers and those you look up to) as well as coaches.

The *third way* is to intentionally staff the jobs or responsibilities that do not require your attention. If you are running a multimillion-dollar company, but still doing the bookkeeping, you are not best using your time.

Your job is to move your entire team forward to accomplish the purpose before you. You cannot do that if you are spending time on things someone else could do.

Rescuing Yourself

As a leader, it is critically important that you learn to manage yourself, your time, energy, and resources by priorities. Otherwise, you will never stop feeling overwhelmed.

You cannot reasonably expect to manage others well if you are unable to manage yourself.

Get clear about your priorities. Do what only you can do. Enable others to do everything else. Get help. If you do these things, you will stop feeling overwhelmed. You will be able to lead into the next inevitable storm with confidence.

Mindsets of Leadership Success

We Define Reality Through the Tinted Lens of Our Perspective

I have consistently been in a leadership or supervisory role since I was a teenager. This has included business startups, nonprofits, and boards.

In these roles, I have had many opportunities to discover my limits. That is, my personal ceilings for my growth, achievement, or success.

I have consulted and coached leaders for nearly twenty years. This has allowed me frequent insight into when others hit their limits.

I've learned a lot about limits—especially about what we perceive to be our limits.

All leaders eventually encounter their limits. We all have limits. Or, something limits us. Sometimes, it does not seem fair.

There is absolutely no question that some people are born into privilege. Others find their way into relationships and social circles, which open unique opportunities. Some just seem blessed as natural leaders.

However, despite apparent advantages, these privileged few experience limits too.

In fact, there exists a consistent and pervasive reality for all of these leaders: Most of our limits are self-constructed.

Your Relationship to Adversity Makes the Difference

When studying leaders, you quickly discover that *adversity* is a common path to leadership. You also discover why nearly all successful entrepreneurs will talk about the need for *courage* and *perseverance*.

Mindset is what makes the difference. Yes, a great financial situation and a solid team helps. But, even in a roaring economy, some leaders will only see obstacles. And, in the weakest of economies, some leaders will still discover opportunities.

Mindsets are not fixed nor binary. You are not stuck one way or the other. We tend to sit on a spectrum. We may even slide around on the spectrum, depending on the situations or circumstances that we face.

The following three mindset areas have the greatest impact on your (and my) future potential and growth.

Growth Mindset Versus Fixed Mindset

A fixed mindset forms the belief that our intelligence, skills, abilities, and opportunities in life are fixed. They are set at birth. Or, by status. Or, whatever.

A growth mindset forms the belief that our intelligence, skills, abilities, and opportunities can be grown or changed. Birth or status provides a starting point. But, it does not determine an endpoint.

I often encounter a fixed mindset in leaders who do not believe in planning or setting a direction for their future. They will say, "We can't know what will happen anyway."

This betrays a belief that they see planning as an attempt to guess at or prophecy a set future—as opposed to being willing to set a course for the desired future. This is indicative of a fixed mindset.

There is a very well-studied phenomenon with students that demonstrates the difference between these mindsets.[1] Students who are told, "You're smart at math," do well until they run into a difficult problem. Being smart/not smart is a *fixed* perception. Since they struggle with the challenge, they believe they aren't naturally smart at this particular task. So, they are more likely to quit trying.

Students who are told, "Wow, you really worked hard at that!" can take on progressively more difficult challenges. This is a *growth* perspective. They believe their effort is what allows them to overcome. As a result, they tend to overcome.

Leaders with a growth mindset are more likely to find solutions, push through challenges, and discover resources and opportunities than their fixed-mindset counterparts.

They experience more success because they believe they can create it.

How to Grow

Here are three tips that will help you develop a growth mindset.

---

[1] Growth Mindset, Learning Mindsets, https://mindsetscholarsnetwork.org/learning-mindsets/growth-mindset/ (accessed April 23, 2019)

1. Relationships

   Surround yourself with people who are growing and bettering themselves. Limit time around people who think from a fixed perspective. The mindsets of the people that you *marinate* yourself in will impact you.

2. Progress Not Perfection

   Personally, one of my biggest breakthroughs in life came with the idea of improving where I was at—as opposed to becoming perfect. A mentor advised me to stop aiming for 100 percent (the target I grew up with) and instead aim for a solid 80 percent. I am not a brain surgeon. And, 80 percent is good enough for most things I do.

   Ironically, not being a perfectionist has resulted in my getting better, faster, at the things that I do. Because I am less worried about mistakes or failure, I am willing to try more, more often. This translates into frequent practice, which leads to growth.

3. Learn a New Skill

   The actual experience of going out and learning something new (particularly if you practice *progress not perfection*) will go a long way to helping you develop a growth mindset. It does not matter if this is a professional skill, a cooking class, or a martial art.

   In fact, if I am coaching a new leader, we sometimes choose a nonwork-related skill as a part of the coaching focus. The skill they choose is not what is important.

   What is important is the ability to ingrain these three success mindsets into a new leader:

   - *I have been successful: I have a history of success. I've proven I can succeed.*
   - *I am successful: What I'm doing, right now, will be successful.*
   - *I will be successful: I am able to succeed at the projects and goals I pursue.*

This is not about magical thinking. It's the simple fact that someone who doesn't believe that they have succeeded, are succeeding or will succeed—likely won't. Success belongs to those who believe they can. It may not always happen (progress not perfection) but it will happen often enough.

To build that mindset, a new leader needs to cultivate a personal inventory of success. The experience of choosing to learn something and then going out and successfully learning it is innately empowering. Becoming stronger, more able, and more confident in one area of your life can benefit all areas of your life.

Ownership Mindset Versus Unaccountability Mindset

Leaders who *own* the consequences of their choices and behaviors empower themselves. Even when this means owning mistakes or failures. The ability to take ownership means you own the ability to grow, to adjust, and to change.

These leaders make their attitudes a choice. The success of their teams is also a choice. One that they own.

Leaders who minimize, rationalize, blame, deflect, or otherwise make excuses *disempower* themselves. This might come from a fatalistic perspective, a weak self-image, or just an unwillingness to take responsibility.

These leaders want choice and may demand that they are given choices. But refuse to consistently own their choices or the consequences.

Leaders who own their own choices and behaviors *and* resulting consequences experience distinct benefits. They are:

- *More able to grow as leaders.* These leaders see cause and effect. They see their leadership as a *causal force.* As they own the effects of their choices, they are better equipped to adapt their behaviors and choices. This allows them to achieve better consequences, more consistently.
- *More able to quickly adapt.* Having ownership does not mean that there are not other forces at work that support or frustrate success. Ownership allows you to see yourself as an actor with these forces, not a victim. These leaders are able to reposition to take advantage of (or create) opportunities. They are able to adjust and avoid threats.
- *More effective at empowering and building their team.* These leaders believe in growth. They believe that the individuals they lead can grow. They are more able to lead, mentor, and coach in a way that assumes and produces growth in those around them.

How to Grow

Here is a simple but powerful way to help you begin to grow an ownership mindset.

Strictly Monitor Your Language

This is your Yoda moment. Talk about what you *did* or *did not* do. Do
not talk about trying (unless you are diagnosing what you could do better
next time). Completely rid yourself of statements like, "I intended to/
meant to/planned to/thought about..."

When you start talking only about what you actually did or didn't do,
you stop excusing not doing things. You start owning what you actually
did. As tough as this might feel to some, it is actually empowering. It is
empowering simply because you start becoming very honest and clear
about your choices and behaviors. This allows you to shape them in ways
that are more effective.

Maybe when giving gifts to family members, "It's the thought that
counts." That is not even remotely true in leadership. What matters, as a
leader, is *what you did or did not do* and *the results of that choice.*

Own your words. Own your choices, actions, and the results. Talking
in these terms is an act of ownership and will help you begin to see yourself as a causal force.

Abundance Mindset Versus Scarcity Mindset

The scarcity mindset is the mindset most people have. Even wealthy
people have it. It dominates (and severely limits) social and political
conversations.

It is the view of life that says that "there is only so much to go around."
It suggests that other people might have *gotten theirs,* but I might not *get
mine.*

It hints that influence, happiness, and contentment are all connected
to things that I either need to fight for or accept that I will never have.

The abundance mindset is not about money or having a lot of stuff.
Otherwise, so many wealthy people would not struggle with still feeling

like they are not financially secure. It is about viewing the world as a place where we can always have enough. A world where we can always create more value, more wealth, or resources. It allows for easy generosity of resources, time, and relationships.

Abundance and scarcity are both about ways of seeing.

A leader who has an abundance mindset believes the market can be grown, new resources can be created or found, and good employees will be recruited or trained. A leader with a scarcity mindset believes that in this market—if they win, we must lose. This leader believes that resources are limited and may be lost forever. That there is *no one* to hire.

It is not that there are not economic ups and downs, difficulty accessing resources, or good staff. But, if your perception is defined by limits and scarcity, you cannot help but play a zero-sum game. Either I win and you lose. Or, you win and I lose.

Even among those who have more than they need, the "dog eat dog" mentality that often controls them is largely driven by the underlying fear that there is not enough.

These following four tips will help you grow from scarcity to abundance.

- *Practice Gratitude*: Identify three things daily you are grateful for. This trains your mind to identify good that you have received.
- *Practice Appreciation*: Identify one thing daily you appreciate about someone else and tell them. This trains you to see other people as sources or producers of value—not only consumers of value.
- *Practice Generosity*: Give your money, time, or resources. Give from the place where you feel tightest. Make a practice of giving to others. This helps confront any inner tendencies to horde. It also allows you to experience what many others have already known that "those who give—receive."
- *Practice Idea Generation*: Many leaders struggle with a scarcity of ideas or a poverty of creativity. This results in a fear that sounds something like this, "If we don't go with this idea, or option, I won't get what I want/need!" This kind of thinking results in very impoverished decision-making.

I do this exercise regularly and advise it to clients: Write down 10 ideas every day. They do not have to be usable, practical, or even reasonable ideas. They just have to be ideas. About anything you want. (I usually pick a theme.) This takes far less time than what most people think. Over time, my clients discover they can whip out 10 new ideas in just a few minutes.

The ability to do this helps you discover that there are many options, many combinations, and many alternatives. This leads to creating value, which leads to abundance.

Growing as a Leader

When you find yourself approaching a limit or a ceiling of any kind, review these mindsets. Explore whether you are holding yourself back in some way. It is definitely possible that there is another force out there placing a limit on you. However, it is far more likely that the force holding you down is one of your own creation.

Why Character Is Key

Did you think the Lord of the Flies was inspiring?

Abraham Lincoln said, "Nearly all men can stand adversity, but if you want to test a man's character, give him power."

I received an e-mail that included a request from a magazine writer. She was looking for thoughts on how male leaders, who were allies to women, could support women in the workplace. This was written during the early part of the early #MeToo movement as it related to Harvey Weinstein and others in Hollywood and Washington.

I responded to her request, but I found myself bothered by the basic premise: That there was a presupposition of a fixed battle between genders in the workplace that requires the existence of allies.

In my mind, any leader *should* be the ally of every employee, regardless of gender, in the pursuit of workplace success and *should* help them all work together.

Yes, conflicts exist. But my answer to the writer's question was: Leaders (of any gender) *should not* allow this kind of conflict to exist. Not in their workplace.

Whether or not you agree with my statement above, here's my actual point: The words *should* and *should not* only have meaning in the context of ethics or morality. I firmly believe that leaders *should* be people of character. They *should* act in the best interests of others.

This does not mean they will. But, when leaders do not, eventually followers feel violated. And, at that point, the leader is no longer leading, but trying to stay in control.

Character is just good business. The science around leadership and organizational dynamics supports the business case that leaders *should be people of character.* The common belief that successful business requires life in gray, ethical murkiness, or outright acceptance of sleight of hand or deceit does not bear out. The often-accepted perspective that "It's not wrong if you can get away with it" does not translate to higher business performance. In fact, the academic literature shows a direct relationship between ethical business practices, corporate social responsibility, and increased profitability.[2]

This is not surprising. But for some reason, cynical or Machiavellian attitudes persist. Many believe you need to cut corners to get ahead. I have often heard, "Sometimes you just have to do business" as a way of explaining an ethically questionable decision.

Think about it. Would you not rather do business with someone you view as trustworthy and conscientious? So would most other people. And, they will. This is not an epiphany.

I recently had a conversation with a senior staffer at a large organization. This organization enjoys national recognition and is award-winning in its field. However, she is wrestling with corruption and lack of internal integrity that runs rampant internally.

I have significant personal experience with this organization. I know for a fact that regardless of awards, their financials, staffing situations, and outcomes are all struggling because of internal character issues. Primarily on the part of senior leaders.

---

[2] Jiang,K., J. Hu, Y. Hong, H. Liao, and S. Liu. 2016. "Do It Well and Do It Right: The Impact of Service Climate and Ethical Climate on Business Performance and the BoundaryConditions." *Journal of Applied Psychology* 101, no. 11, pp. 1553–1568. https://psycnet.apa.org/record/2016-37463-001

Their tree may look fine on the outside. But, it is rotting in its core. If they do not change, they will not be able to withstand a real storm.

All other things being equal, ethical organizations will perform better over the long run.

Why Is Corruption or Abuse of Power Tolerated?

I have worked in places where sexual harassment and other kinds of abuses of power were common. In terms of sexual harassment, I have experienced it myself. Two times from women in positions of authority or seniority. Once from a man.

Probably like you, I have experienced or observed many other kinds of abuses of power as well.

In nearly all of these cases, others stayed silent.

The reasons were not far different from what recently has come to light with Harvey Weinstein or the others:

- The people who have the power to help are the people misusing their power.
- Others are complicit. They know what is going on, but feel they have something to lose and nothing to gain by speaking up on behalf of others.
- Everyone else acts like it is normal—so it is easy to think it should be related to as normal. The abuser is enabled.
- The abuses of power can be subtle. It is not always easy to identify or point out what exactly happened, and it is often only in hindsight that the pattern becomes evident.
- Many abusers are skilled manipulators, reframing their behaviors as understandable or excusable or at least deserving of being overlooked. They often target people less likely to speak up.
- The fear of loss or retribution is greater than the belief in justice.
- There may be shame. Someone feels shame at what happened, or choices they made—or fear that something else they have done will be exposed if they come forward.

Why Is This So Prevalent?

Lord Acton, a nineteenth century author and Cambridge professor, penned the famous thought, "Power corrupts. Absolute power corrupts absolutely. Great men are almost always bad men..."

I understand the observation, but I do not agree with his conclusion or his understanding of cause and effect.

Instead, I am inclined to agree with George Bernard Shaw's statement: "Power does not corrupt men; fools, however, if they get into a position of power, corrupt power."

That is the problem: Power, like a drug, reduces social inhibitions. It amplifies existent character. If you have character problems, Dr. Jekyll is set aside. Mr. Hyde feels free to do as he wills.

If you have power, particularly if you've internalized power as part of your self-image, you are naturally less inhibited. When we are less inhibited, our true character is more likely to show. In fact, it is likely to be magnified or amplified.

Power, like money, is an amplifier. If you have good character, power will amplify that. If you have poor character, power will amplify that.

Our struggle is not with power. It is with ourselves.

The Real Question

Is it safe to magnify our character? To let what is in us—out?

As leaders, do we actively cultivate our character?

What do we do when we start to see ourselves acting out? Acting out is not limited to sexual harassment or assault.

Perhaps we act out with impatience, anger, self-protection, vengeance, jealousy, or any of the other very real base motivations that rattle around in each of us. As leaders, we are real people, with real stuff going on inside of us. If we are honest, it is not all pretty. The question is not, "Are you perfect?" The question is, "Are you working on your stuff?"

Do we value character enough to make our own character development a priority?

What Is Character?

So, what is character? What does it mean to be a person or leader of character? What does it mean to build an organization of character?

My belief is that leadership character is principally reflected in my answers to the question: "How do I treat others? Particularly those with less influence or power than myself?"

This is a rewording of the golden rule: "Do unto others as you would have them do unto you."

Consider these four areas of application:

- **How do I protect, increase, or at least not damage the dignity or worth of others?** How do I act so that at a minimum, I am not robbing others of their dignity? Ideally, can I help them step into living a life with a greater sense of personal worth and value?
- **How do I provide, advance, or at least not threaten the sense of safety or security of others?** Leaders have power. Employers have power. How do we use that so that others have room to live at peace? Even when we need to confront poor behavior or make hard and painful decisions—do we do this in a way to protect others as much as possible? (I am not referring to preventing people from experiencing natural consequences of poor decisions. However, in those situations, a leader of character will attempt to coach, grow, or encourage the person in question.)
- **How do I support the growth of others or at least not inhibit it?** The author and thinker Robert Greenleaf said it best. "The best test as a leader is: Do those served grow as persons; do they become healthier, wiser, freer, more autonomous, more likely themselves to become leaders?"
- **How do I bring value to others?** One of the great traps of leadership (and a great exposé of personal character) is the belief that, "I've made it to the top of the heap. Now everyone serves me, my vision, my desires!" Instead, the most impactful leaders—in terms of producing the greatest amount of

good—are focused on providing as much value as possible to those that they led. They see their positions as vehicles of service. Not a throne from which to be served.

It is my belief that as any leader answers these questions (or even better, asks others to answer these questions about them), it will provide an accurate litmus test of character.

When considering this, remember character is not like the medieval practice of buying indulgences or the contemporary practice of buying carbon tax credits. I can't tell the truth two times to make up for one lie. Or follow through three times to make up for the two contracts I didn't complete. Or that I, on purpose, didn't cheat at least 60 percent of the time.

There is not a scale. It's not about being more.

Character is about integrity, consistency, and alignment. You either are trustworthy—or people don't trust you.

The Challenge

Remember the story I told at the beginning of the book? The one where I ask a class to describe what a "*leader*" is? The typical responses are often reflections of a leader's character.

People are looking for leaders with character.

Leaders, with character, match up with what people intrinsically believe is right. When we do this, they naturally start to follow. At that point, leadership becomes easy.

PART II

Seven Essential Executive Skills

CHAPTER 3

The Skills of Creating Purpose

Effective leadership is not about making speeches or being liked; leadership is defined by results not attributes.

—Peter F. Drucker

The Seven Essential Skills of Leadership

Ultimately, leaders need to be able to produce results. To do so requires the use of seven specific skills, which we will explore in the next three chapters. These skills fall under three categories: The Skills of Creating Purpose, The Skills of Building People, and The Skills of Persuasion.

Most leaders put more effort into redesigning a logo than clarifying what they are trying to accomplish and why it matters.

Skill #1: Thinking Strategically

All men can see these tactics whereby I conquer, but what none can see is the strategy out of which victory is evolved.

—Sun Tzu

My best clients lead well. They grow regardless of the economy. They thrive despite challenges. Sure, they face setbacks. But, in the big picture, they are examples of the ability to consistently accomplish the goals they value and pursue.

What do they share in common? They have leaders who think strategically.

What Is Strategy?

Strategy, in essence, is a framework for making decisions or setting goals. It is a framework based on defined values and priorities.

If building a house, a strategy might look like:

"We'd like to build a highly energy efficient house, within a certain budget, that can be completed in a certain time frame, is built for hosting guests, has individual space for all family members and has a rustic look."

That simple statement combines a new homebuilder's values and priorities and can easily be used to guide decision making.

Strategy is flexible. Plans are rigid. There are many plans (or blueprints) that can be created with this strategy. They can be changed as new opportunities or challenges emerge—but even those changes can be guided by the overall strategy.

The plan, or the blueprint, is not the strategy.

Leaders who think strategically have developed a decision-making framework for themselves and their organization. They are disciplined in its use. They work the strategy, even if the plans are updated or altered.

Effective leaders exercise five strategic practices:

1. Use your values and vision to clarify your focus and build.
2. Cultivate organizational self-awareness.
3. Cultivate external awareness.
4. Engage both strategic and operational priorities.
5. Disciplined implementation.

Strategic Practice #1: Use Your Values and Vision to Clarify and Build

Strategic leaders develop a very clear sense of two things:

- Values: What is important to us and why?
- Vision: What are we trying to create and why?

It is not necessary that your answers to these questions be framed in a way that fits on a bumper sticker, rolls off the tongue, or looks good on a website.

It is necessary that your answers make sense to you and provide practical guidance for decision-making.

To illustrate, imagine that a leadership team is facing a decision about expanding services into new geography. On the face of it, the idea might be exciting or scary. It might be high or low risk. It might have questionable value or a high reward. It might be a lot of things.

A strategic leader will ask questions, such as the ones below, by referencing the values and the vision:

- Does expanding or not expanding help us better express or stay consistent with our values?
- Does expanding or not expanding better help us move toward our vision?
- If we expand, how do we do so in such a way as to better express or stay consistent with our values?
- If we expand, how do we do so in such a way as to advance our vision?

This can and should be applied to goal-setting, the development of new products and services, hiring processes, staff development and discipline processes, policy development, and so on.

By always referencing your values and vision, you start to direct all of your energy and resources toward your priorities. Now you are thinking strategically.

Strategic Practice #2: Cultivate Organizational Self-Awareness

One of the things that I look for when I work with leaders and organizations is the degree of consistency between how they describe themselves and what is actually experienced by others.

If there is a high level of consistency, even when describing problem behaviors, there is usually a high probability that we can accomplish a successful change.

However, if leadership in an organization tends toward a lack of awareness or denial, it is difficult to do productive work.

Strategic leaders pay attention to how their leadership is experienced and its efficacy. They are aware of their priorities, the primary value their organization provides, and how it does so. They keep tabs on, innovate with, and continually improve the effectiveness of their operations.

Strategic Practice #3: Cultivate External Awareness

Strategic leaders pay attention to the environment.

To their industry, to trends, to demography, to the economy, to politics, and to what is happening around them.

They do not make the mistake of ignoring and thereby getting surprised or overwhelmed by external forces. They also do not make the mistake of being passive and believing they are unable to position themselves for opportunities or to mitigate difficulties.

The best leaders are watching what happens around them and wonder, *How can we benefit from this?* or *What new value can we bring to others because of this?* or *What do we need to defend against in this situation?*

They engage their environment.

Strategic Practice #4: Engage Both Strategic and Operational Priorities

Some attribute to Napoleon the quote, "An army marches on its belly." The overt meaning is that an infantry needs to be well-fed or you will not succeed in your campaign.

The underlying meaning is that you need to pay attention to operations, logistics, the daily, and maybe even mundane if you are to achieve success that will be sustained.

In fact, George Washington's success in the Revolutionary War is attributed to his ability to excel operationally and logistically.

Many organizations pursue strategy at the cost of operational excellence or consistency. That is like building an addition to your house while allowing your foundation to be eaten away from under you. You need to have clear priorities for both strategy and operations.

Strategic Practice #5: Disciplined Implementation

As mentioned earlier, planning does not make you strategic. A plan does nothing on its own. It does not implement itself.

Leaders have to complete their plans to be strategic.

They do not leave implementation to chance. They approach it with intent and determination. They constantly refer to values and vision. Everything is grounded in and tested by those.

They ensure that leadership within the organization provides accountability and consistency throughout the organization. They ensure that there is sufficient skill and capacity to implement.

They make it happen.

Strategic Thinking Can Be Practiced by Individuals and Teams

Because this is a framework and a process for decision-making and priority-setting, anyone can learn to be a strategic thinker.

This is not a skill only reserved for those few people *born* as strategists.

Teams grow in their ability to think strategically through practice and regular cycles of thinking through the steps mentioned above. In my experience, it takes most teams at least two or three strategic cycles to really find their stride.

This is because of the learning curve along the way. Typically, the questions they learn to answer look like:

How do we set clearer goals that everyone understands the same way? (Goals can be mushy and it is hard to know what success looks like.)

What are our individual roles and responsibilities? (There are often assumptions, gaps, or overlap.)

- How do we adapt when something unexpected happens? (A change in the environment, an inaccurate assumption, a significant challenge.)
- What behaviors do we all need to agree to be successful? (It is common that a new set of habits are required to achieve a new level of success or accomplishment.)

- How do we hold each other accountable? (How do we build sufficient trust and respect that allows us to have hard conversations?)

As you incorporate these practices into your decision-making habits, you will find that you and your team will increasingly become strategic thinkers.

Skill #2: Value Creation

People will always be attracted to what they value.

What the Best Leaders and Salespeople Have in Common

You can get everything in life you want if you will just help enough other people get what they want.

—Zig Ziglar

One winter, in college, I went with a girlfriend to help her buy a car. We went into the dealership, explained what we were looking for, and in what price range.

"I've got just the thing!" says the salesman.

Then, he took us out into the lot. He started selling her a totally different vehicle than what we asked for.

He was almost successful. In snowy, freezing weather, he pointed out a lime green jeep with a removable top. He started describing the image of carefree driving, in any road condition, with the wind in her hair.

She was hooked. She wanted it. For a moment.

Of course, it was not what she was looking for. Or in her price range. What he showed us was nice, but it was not what she asked for or even was in a position to buy.

No sale.

Years later, my wife needed a new car as our family was growing. I went to a different dealership this time. Continental Auto Group.

They asked me a lot of questions about what I was looking for. I told them. They said, "Give us a couple days."

A couple days later, I got a call.

I went in. What I was looking for was parked by the entrance. I was told to take it home for a few days and see if we really wanted it.

There was no pitch. They just found what I wanted and made sure I was happy with it.

I bought it immediately. They helped shuttle it to my house.

They made the sale because they went out of their way to find out what I wanted and then provide it.

Great Leadership is Very Much Like a Great Sales Experience

What is unique about the most successful organizations? What is it that all effective leaders do?

They create and provide more value than you expect.

It does not matter what kind of organization you lead. If you do not offer something that others need or desire, your efforts are irrelevant.

It is a critical leadership skill, a critical skill for executives or owners, to ensure they create and provide value throughout their organizations.

What Is Value?

True value is in the eye of the beholder. Your beholders include customers, employees, shareholders, investors, vendors, and partners. They do not all want the same thing.

Therefore, get to know your beholders and what they value.

This is not always easy to do. Many people do not think much about this. They might not know how to tell you what they want. So ask and listen: Frame your question in different ways. Observe behavior. Listen to casual conversaions. Learn what they want.

We all have done this in a dating relationship. We observe and learn all about the person whose attention we hope to hold. And, now that I am married with small children, I work to understand what my wife and children really want—which is regularly evolving.

What others value must be discovered. Once you find it and offer to meet that desire, most of your work is done.

More Than Ever Leaders Need to Understand What Their Employees Value

If you don't, you will always struggle with getting and holding employees. Definitely with getting and holding ideal employees (as ideal employees want and value different things than average employees).

I was sitting in a fancy office in a fancy building with a well-dressed leader.

She asked, "How do I motivate people?"

"You can't," I said. "You can only find out what motivates them already and learn to connect to that. Once you learn to tie into what they are already motivated by, they'll be engaged. If what they are motivated by doesn't tie into their work responsibilities, they aren't a good fit."

She looked crestfallen.

I do not know what she was hoping for as an answer. Maybe a change in a compensation program.

That is often what executives assume.

But, what was needed was for her to lead differently.

She needed to learn to figure out, "Where is that employee at—internally? In their motivation? How do I get them to willingly offer their energy and skills to accomplish something we both want?"

That takes a little bit of effort.

Many leaders check out at this point. "Don't tell me I need to lead! Tell me I can change an HR policy!"

What Is Motivation?

Motivation is an internal drive or desire that I feel. That you feel. That your team feels.

It is inside. It compels me, you, and others to act.

We all, naturally, begin to look for ways to act that allow us to increase the likelihood of having that desire realized.

As most people have multiple desires, they may be willing to subduct some. For a time. But, as options make themselves available, their deeper desires will start to emerge.

Out of college, I worked for a Swiss humanitarian organization called Medair. To join, they conducted a 10-day screening/training that everyone needed to go through to be *considered* for a position.

To attend, I had to apply. If accepted, I had to take time off, fly to Switzerland (on my tab), and *pay* to go through their recruitment process to see if I could get selected.

During the 10-day process, we went through training where we listened to experienced staff tell stories of physical hardship, challenge, discouragement, frustration, and sacrifice.

Then, they put us through a simulated crisis where they worked us, deprived us of sleep, and stressed us as much as they could to see if they thought we could hack it. Only 20 percent or so of those who attended would be offered positions. And then, the first year in that position would be as a volunteer. Unpaid.

It was the biggest anti-sell ever.

And, it was extraordinarily effective. Highly trained doctors, nurses, engineers, and executives of Fortune 500 companies were all trying to pass the test to prove that they were good enough—to work for free in an uncomfortable, insecure environment.

What made it work?

They tapped, directly, into what was really motivating us. At a deep level.

- Do you want to make a real difference in the world?
- Do you want to change a child's life?
- Do you want to be a hero to someone?
- Do you want to wake up every day feeling like your life has purpose?

They supplied the value. Highly skilled people, with options, were literally paying for the opportunity to be considered.

It Is Not Primarily About Money

Money is almost never the answer. Studies repeatedly show this. Too many leaders refuse to believe this.

Money matters for people who are struggling to meet basic needs. Although it isn't really money they want as much as security. It matters to people whose work clearly adds to the bottom line. Although it isn't really money they want as much as equity and recognition. For nearly everyone, money is just a symbol. A symbol for being able to achieve something of deeper value.

Higher performing employees tend to have a clearer sense of this than average employees.

What Actually Motivates People? At a Deep Level?

Three things:

1. *Significance*: People want to feel important. That life has value. That their work or contribution has purpose.
2. *Security*: People want to feel financially, relationally, and physically secure.
3. *Satisfaction*: People want to enjoy life and the relationships around them.

What Medair did not offer in the way of the normal definition of security, it made up for in truckloads by offering significance and satisfaction.

- Every single day, you will be living a life of purpose.
- People will stop dying because of you.
- People will have hope because of you.
- You (might) get to be a hero.
- You will meet amazing people and experience what others only read about.

Powerful Stuff

Higher pay does not to a great job of retaining staff on its own. Especially not ideal employees. Not if it leaves a deficit in what people really want.

Many executives miss this. It is a costly and common mistake.

As a result, they struggle with turnover. Or, they retain their staff, but their staff is not ideal. Or, their shareholders never seem content. Or, their customers are fickle.

Here is one example: Let us consider the average shareholder who sits on a board of a medium-sized company.

Sure, they want a financial return on their investment.

But, if they are purely driven for a financial return, they would not so frequently make the kinds of decisions that frustrate financial success.

What drivers are involved in their decision-making?

- They might like saying they are the owner of a company.
- They might like the perception of status or power.
- They might like the deference they are shown by a respected industry leader.
- They might like the board meetings in Vegas.
- They might like the intellectual challenge of running a business.
- They might be looking for interesting ways to fill their time.

My point is, money, on its own, is not what drives them. It is not the sole value they seek. But, they might use financial terms to describe it.

Who Should Value Be Created for and Offered to?

Short answer: As many people as possible.

What really motivates your leadership or management team?

What about your staff?

What is it that your customers are really looking for?

What about your shareholders?

What about partners, suppliers, or vendors?

What is it you really want?

The more value you create and provide to each of these groups, the more successful your leadership will be.

This is about tapping into their motivation. Their sense of drive. Their sense of *what makes it worth it.*

When you know that, and offer that, leadership becomes easy. Success becomes easy.

How to Use Value to Hire and Retain the Best Employees and Strongest Leadership Team

Employees who wake up in the morning looking forward to their day, do so because they do *meaningful work with leaders they respect* and *people they like.*

Ideal employees (motivated, creative, ethical) nearly always have choices of where to work. And as long as they do, compensation alone will not attract them.

However, it will attract plenty of non ideal employees who are either only motivated for mercenary reasons (and may quickly turn over) or do not have options elsewhere (and may not turn over fast enough).

Question to ask yourself:

- What kind of people do you attract to work for you?
- Who is not applying (or accepting) that you wish would?
- Why do your ideal employees stay? Why do they leave?

How to Use Value to Attract Your Ideal Customers

There are many ways to slice the psychological pie of what drives customer behavior. However, there are two primary starting points:

1. They have a need or are dissatisfied: What is their unfulfilled need or unmet desire?
2. They hope for transformation or fulfillment: What is the change they hope for?

To the degree that your products or services are viewed as uniquely valuable is the degree to which they are more attractive to others. Commodity services or products are not viewed as valuable in and of themselves. They are traded purely on price—which pushes value down.

Commodity Services or Products

At the most basic level, I drive *past* two gas stations to get to the one I most often use. I pass the first because it is difficult to cross traffic to get to it. I pass the second one because, for several times in a row, their machines would not read my credit card or were out of order. So, now I do not bother.

Gas is a commodity. I cannot tell the difference between their gas and the gas across the street. As long as the machines work, my experience at the pump is nearly always the same, no matter what brand I'm using.

I'll use whoever's is most convenient. I have no gas loyalty.

Specialty Services

Coffee is a commodity. But it can be turned into a specialty.

I am a regular customer of a local coffee company called Kaladi Brothers Coffee. At the most basic level, I am willing to pay more for a cup of coffee that tastes better and is made by a company that treats me well and also actively finds ways to contribute to the community.

They choose their beans and blends carefully. The staff is consistent and well-trained. They know who I am. They look out for me. A drink may even be waiting for me as I arrive to pay for it. I am occasionally invited into cuppings or to offer my opinion on new coffees they are considering. Their product and the service are unique and superior.

I can tell the difference between their product and service and anywhere else I go. It is specialized. If I go to a competitor, even a quality competitor, I know I will not have the same experience—even if the experience is positive.

As a result, I have been a consistent customer of theirs for decades.

- Do you know what your customers want? Or, are you assuming?
- Is there a way to give them more of what they want?
- Is there a way to meet related desires or needs?
- Are you offering commodity services? What value could you offer that would differentiate you?

- Are you offering specialized services? How do you know what your customer is looking for?

How to Use Value to Satisfy Your Shareholders, Employers, or Board

I once sat down with a client to establish the goals of our coaching relationship.

He was very prepared. He wanted to generate one million U.S. dollars a year in personal income. He explained all the ways this was going to happen.

I asked him, "What does that number mean to you?"

He was stumped.

He did not need one million dollars a year. That number was symbolic.

Then, he got emotional. Nearly started crying. And, he told me everything he hoped to accomplish in the next chapter of his life.

One million dollars a year would make that dream possible. Or so he believed.

His real goal was not one million dollars. It was the dream. The money was a method to get to the dream. It could be possible to work hard and achieve the one million and miss the dream. But, he did not need one million dollars to experience his dream.

I knew my work was to help him build the dream. One million dollars may or may not be the method we would use.

Figure out what the dream is of your shareholders, your employers, your board, or anyone else you report to.

Ask them questions like:

- Where would they like to be in five or 10 years?
- What do they hope this will accomplish for the company? For them?
- How do they see what we are doing now contributing to that future goal?
- What makes this important to you?
- What happens if this is not accomplished?

Then you will start to find out (or get hints) what they really want.

Before anyone becomes a client, I spend a significant amount of time with them making sure I know exactly what that individual wants. I explore what makes this important. I want to understand what a lack of success in this area would mean to them. I try to zero in on the value they are looking for.

This helps me target my work more effectively. It helps me connect to the needs of my client.

In some cases, it lets us both know whether I can actually meet those needs. Sometimes I cannot be or I am not the right person. It is better to know that upfront.

It is a big part of why most of my business comes from repeat clients and referrals. Because I was able to focus on what they really wanted and needed. What was valuable to them.

I work to identify the value my customers want and allow that to calibrate my focus and efforts throughout the engagement.

How about you?

What unique value does your leadership produce?

What are one or two ways that you might be able to get a better sense of what value might be wanted or appreciated?

What are one or two ways that you might create or provide a little more value?

Value is a solid business investment.

CHAPTER 4

The Skills of Building People

Neither teams nor people are built in workshops.

Skill #3: Team Building without Trust Falls

The most successful leaders know how to build teams. They know that their efforts are only as effective as their team.

High-performing executives must be able to build and maintain a high-performing team. It is an area of sustained focus. Teamwork is not a pit stop reluctantly taken when problems can no longer be tolerated.

In fact, these leaders do not just build a team. They architect a team. They craft it. They nurture it. They train it.

But, they do not use trust falls.

In fact, team-building rarely occurs in an actual event.

The primary exception to this is for brand new teams. Specifically, people who do not already know each other or have a history of working together. In these instances, an induction or orientation process can be helpful to quickly build rapport, initiate trust, and establish common norms and expectations.

However, apart from new teams: A team is built through *how you lead*.

Five Leadership Practices That Build Teams

There are five basic leadership practices, that when utilized, will create a high-performing team:

- Actively leading
- Adjusting leadership styles to best fit the need
- Creating clarity in purpose and direction

- Engaging the commitment of others
- Consistently providing accountability for performance and behavior

There are precious few leaders who seem to just naturally know how to do these things. For most people in leadership, it is more of a mixed bag. Some leaders are very hard workers but not focused. Others have very clear goals, but do not know how to engage the commitment of others.

If you find that you are bumping against a limit of some kind, it is likely a challenge in one of these five practices.

As I help leaders with exit or succession strategies, it is clear that the full price of these challenges is often deferred. It is payable upon the leader's exit—with a lower than desired sales price for the company, a longer than desired exit, a fumbled succession, a complicated legacy or reputation, and so on.

This is no small thing. Less than 30 percent of privately held businesses successfully sell or survive an ownership succession.

Your Ship Needs a Captain: Active Leadership

When it comes to active leadership, there are three common errors that leaders make:

- Being a boss instead of a leader
- Being a friend instead of a leader
- Focusing on the position instead of leading

Active leaders look ahead. They facilitate the growth and engagement of their people. They build and refine their organization. They pay attention to likely needs of their customers.

By contrast, passive leaders may try to *lead* by paying attention to lagging indicators. It is akin to driving by primarily paying attention to the rear-view mirror. They these leaders avoid dealing with issues until they have grown are no longer able to be ignored.

This does not mean that they do not have vision, or are not nice people, or have the ability to organize. But, active leaders *get out in front* of issues, opportunities, needs, or challenges and forge the path forward.

Active leaders are more likely to attract, build, and retain *other active leaders* to be a part of their team.

Matching Your Style to the Team

A team, at the minimum, is a group of people with a shared purpose and reward. The less a group of people shares a purpose or reward, the less they really are a team.

I like to use a sports analogy to describe this. In high school, I played basketball and ran on track and field. Both were teams. But, very different kinds of teams.

Basketball teams win together or lose together. There is a strongly shared purpose and reward. Track and field teams can win or lose together. But the individual can win alone. Not surprisingly, there is a higher emphasis placed on the performance of the individual. There is a weaker shared purpose and reward.

This difference changes how you should lead.

I serve on the board of directors for a non profit that has nine diverse programs. The need for a strong *team* and what that team needs to do changes depending on where you focus within the organization.

There does need to be a strong executive team. This is their *basketball* team. Effective leadership, for the executive team, will spend more time focusing on trust, interpersonal relationships, communication, and clarity around shared goals and differentiated roles and responsibilities.

However, each of the program directors are essentially athletes in different events. They are a *track and field* team. The success or challenges of one program won't necessarily impact another program. To lead program directors effectively requires a focus on helping them set individual program performance goals that are aligned with larger organizational goals while looking for ways to collaborate and support other programs. But, there should be a recognition that one program's success may be very isolated from another's challenges.

Teams that should be *basketball teams* need more active work on alignment, trust-building, and communication. They know they are a team—but proximity and interdependence allow for more friction and frustration. The executive's focus is usually on helping them relate and work well with each other. Clarity about smaller level expectations becomes more important.

Teams that should be *track and field teams* often do not depend on each other for success. It sometimes is not as clear to them that they are a team. This can create silos and a departmental sense of not helping the greater cause because "it's not my job." The executive needs to help this team identify a shared sense of identify and purpose. This includes helping them find ways they can support each other, synergize with each other, and avoid competition for resources.

Creating Alignment Fast: Purpose and Clear Vision

When speaking on team alignment, I have often used the example of how someone loses strength when their spine is unaligned and they have no focus. I will bring a volunteer to the front and have them extend their arm in front of them and look up at the ceiling. Then, I can easily bend their arm.

They were out of alignment and had no focus.

Next, I quickly teach them how to organize their spine so that it is in alignment. Then, I instruct them to find a focal point on a far wall and point their hand toward it. Now, I try to bend their arm—and it is difficult. Sometimes, not possible.

Alignment and focus. It creates strength in our bodies. It will create strength on your team, regardless of the kind of team it is.

Help your team identify its *Why*. Clarify their shared vision or results of success. This is a focus point. Then, align their priorities underneath it. Define which metrics will help you track continued alignment and progress. Help the team describe what they need from each other to stay aligned.

Team alignment is no more complicated than that.

Getting Commitment: Tapping into Motivation and Dependability

I have already written about motivation. But, the topic is critical enough to mention, briefly, again.

Sometimes, I am asked to provide a motivational speech. The belief being, "Can you say something that will create a little boost in everyone?" But, you cannot put motivation into people.

Really, all a motivational speaker can do is identify or address common areas of motivation *already in* his or her audience. Then, the speaker talks about how those desires or motivations can be fulfilled. People are reminded of their vision and passions. Their hope is renewed. They get excited or *motivated*.

But, they will stop being excited if they cannot connect to those areas of motivation when they go back to work. If their work causes them to lose sight of their vision and passion, you will lose their motivation.

A good leader does the same thing as a motivational speaker. Perhaps not through a speech. But, they remind people of what drives them and help them see how that drive can be satisfied through the workplace.

If forming a team, screen for motivation. If people are not motivated by the kinds of things that are easy to align with your goals, they just will not be a good fit on your team. It does not matter how skilled or experienced they are; they need to be excited about the kinds of things that matter in your organization.

If working with an existing team, identify what drives the choices and engagement of those you lead. The more you can create a connection between what they really desire and how it can be fulfilled on this team, the more you have their engagement.

Provide Accountability for Performance and Behavior

It is easier to make small adjustments, then large ones. Effective leaders hold individuals and teams accountable for both performance and behavior. They do not wait for problems to grow. Too many leaders wait too long and problems have become too big.

If there are performance issues, then bring coaching, correction, or resources to bear. If there are behavior issues, correct them. Clarify the needed behaviors. If someone will not change, do not tolerate it for long. If it is a question of skill or aptitude, help find a better position of them. If it is a question of ethics or behaviors, and they will not change, cut them loose.

Any team that has continuous struggles with behaviors or performance has a leadership issue. Not a team issue.

Bringing It Together

Which of these five practices are strengths of yours? How have those strengths brought benefit?

What of these five practices do you need to grow in? What will be the impact if there is no growth?

Often times, just paying attention to a neglected leadership practice helps you grow. In my experience, leaders can grow and make measurable progress within months.

Skill #4: Capacity-Building

Building great people is one of your highest return investments.

Four Secrets All Leaders Need to Know about Growing People

How do you measure leadership effectiveness?

There are several simple ways to do this. One of the best ways is to look at the people nearest to the leader.

Are they growing?

Are they growing in confidence? In ability? In mindset? In capacity?

Are they more able to lead themselves? Are they more able to grow others?

The most effective executives grow the people around them personally and professionally. This is natural for them. A habit. A practice. It comes from a personal sense of delight in seeing others grow and succeed.

Lesser leaders will often demand growth from others—without knowing how to support it. Others feel threatened when others grow. So, they find ways to limit growth.

But, great leaders love seeing the growth of others. They love helping others grow. They will often say that this is one of the most rewarding parts of their work.

Because of this, people around them do grow. Because people grow—the organization grows. It is a natural progression.

Leaders Who Grow Others Exhibit These Four Traits: Humility, Self-Management, Asking More Than Telling, and an Abundance Mentality

Humility

Even though most people dislike arrogance, they are not sure if they like humility either. Consider the following phrases:

- Humble looking
- Humble home
- Humble ambitions
- Humble career

The word *humble* does not seem to do any favors as an adjective.

We do not really know what humility is. We are not sure it sounds good. We do not talk about it much. No one teaches how to *do* humility. Therefore, we do not tend to know how to become humble, how to maintain it, or how to practice it, particularly if we have any level of drive or ambition.

I will suggest that humble leadership embraces strong ambitions. But, it differs from arrogance in the focus of those ambitions. It uses a different *measuring stick* than arrogance. Humble leadership has two primary characteristics:

- *Focusing your efforts for the benefit of others.* Being more passionate about the success of the whole than personal attention or rewards.

- *Using internal measures of success instead of comparative measures.* Defining your success by the value you provide others and how you grew whatever and whomever was around you. *Not* by comparing yourself to others.

These two characteristics allow for high levels of ambition, drive, and success but are focused differently.

Self-Management

Leaders who manage their own time, priorities, and compulsions can grow others. A leader who cannot manage his or her time, priorities, or compulsions will always be led by the urgencies defined by someone else. Someone in a leadership position who does not practice self-management is not actually leading. Instead, they are led by circumstances and other people's problems.

This kind of leader will always find it difficult to stay focused long enough to nurture and build someone else.

Ask More Than Tell

Many leaders like to wax eloquent about the wisdom they have gathered from the lofty heights of their success. Actually, I like to do this. Here I am writing this book. It is an easy trap to fall into. When you are an expert, people ask you to do this. They pay you to do it. This can sound impressive, but it is not the best way to generate actual growth in others.

However, someone who can ask great questions, explore the thinking of others, and spur deeper reflection will generate growth. This requires the ability to *not* be the answer or the resource. But to trust that the person you are growing can discover the answer if asked the right questions.

It requires a capacity to understand what is needed so growth can be obtained. Some of this is related to skill development. But far more is related to mindset development.

Abundance Mentality

Leaders who grow others have a mentality of abundance. They are not trying to get as much of the pie as they can. They are interested in baking more pies. Or starting pie bakeries. Or franchising pie bakeries.

At their very core, they believe they can create whatever pie they need. And they work to do just that. Most people never understand this. So, they fixate on a particular slice of pie, or how many slices of pie are left, or who received the slice they thought they should get.

Growth is not possible from a perspective that is defined by limits rather than possibilities. If you have that perspective, you cannot grow others. I have watched many organizations restrict their own growth because owners or senior leaders feel like they cannot afford to invest in their people. Or they do not have a large enough vision for upcoming high performers to find a place within.

How to Grow Others: Focus on These Four Areas for Development

There are four basic areas a leader who grows others needs to focus on.

1. Grow the Person

Depending on where you are starting from, this can mean different things.

But largely, it boils down to helping people clarify priorities and make faster and better decisions through those priorities.

When someone knows how to make decisions, they naturally become more confident. Confidence, when supported by good decisions and the ability to follow through, will take people a long way.

Too many people do not have enough confidence. Or they have undeserved confidence. Great leaders grow people who have earned the confidence they exhibit.

2. Give Them Experience

It was in college where I learned that internships and practicums were often worth more than the degree. The actual experiences and the relationships built during the internship brought more value and opened up more opportunities than just being able to claim a diploma.

Give your people new experiences. Allow them to face new challenges. Expose them to opportunities, relationships, and the behind-the-scenes machinations of how things are done.

Too many people come into leadership only seeing what is presented from the *stage*. Allow your people to be involved behind the scenes. They will grow.

3. Develop Their Skills

Invest in the skill development of others. The more your people can do and the more confident they are in doing it, the better everyone is.

Identify relevant skills for where they are in their journey *and* for where they are headed. Ensure that they are equipped and experienced in the use of those skills so that they can thrive.

4. Provide Contextual Knowledge

As a consultant, I nearly always work in situations where I start with very little context. I usually know very little about the history, situation, relationships, or subtext that have developed over time. As someone who has often worked cross-culturally, I know context can be difficult to discern or interpret. This limits effective work. It increases the likelihood of creating resistance or errors.

Over time, I have learned how to quickly unearth and infer context. I have learned how to draw that information out of others. I have learned how to trust my instincts regarding what I should pay attention to, but to verify before taking action.

This is a difficult skill. Most people do not have to constantly navigate that new contexts. As a result, most people do not have the experience to do it well. So, when someone is new to your organization or project or team, provide them with context. Take the time to explain *why* and to connect the dots.

Just because the lights are on for you does not mean they are on for everyone else. Help others understand how to navigate a new situation or terrain.

Personal Development Translates into Developing Others

Your own personal development translates in your leadership development. The more you invest in personal growth, the more the growth of others will be a natural consequence. One naturally follows the other. Simple methods for growth that are accessible to nearly anyone include:

- Find mentors
- Surround yourself with others who are and do what you want to be and do
- Hire a coach
- Read books, listen to podcasts, or otherwise immerse yourself in content relevant to your growth
- Get a counselor

Do whatever it is you need to do to keep growing as a person. Do not leave your growth to chance or happy accident. Ensure it. That will ensure the growth of those around you.

Growing Others Will Make You a Better Leader

Every good coach and consultant I know loves their job, in part, because the better they are at helping others grow, the more they grow themselves.

There is a very direct relationship between the two. It is a virtuous circle, ever looping upward. Helping others grow helps you grow yourself. As you grow yourself, you are more able to help others grow.

What Is Next for You?

- What is one area where you would like to grow? What is one step you can take to ensure that growth happens?

Who is someone that you would like to help grow? What is one step you can take to help that person grow this week?

Skill #5: How to Turn Around a Team That Struggles

If Not You, Who? If Not Now, When?

—Alan Weiss

Pre-Ownership

I had my first job when I was 15. I was a courtesy clerk. A bag boy. I carried customer's groceries at a local grocery store. I hated bagging groceries. If I got lucky, I got to chase stray carts around the parking lot and herd them back to the store. I would wander far and wide, searching for stray carts. Anything to delay coming back to the store.

Actually, I just hated working. I hated *having* to do things. For my next few jobs, I looked for opportunities that seemed to require the least amount of effort. I will be honest. I was nobody's model employee. I felt no ownership for my work or reputation.

Ownership

When I was 19, I helped start a coffee shop with two other friends. It was an enormous amount of work. I was involved in everything. I worked all the time. I basically lived at work.

I loved it.

I also had staff. I managed roughly 30 people. Suddenly, I began to understand the frustrations previous managers had expressed toward me.

"Ohhhh, that's why (being thorough, getting things done on time, not hiding in the back, being friendly) matters!"

I had never known. I felt ownership. It changed my life.

Creating Ownership and Accountability

One of the greatest leadership accomplishments is the ability to create a *culture of ownership and accountability.*

As a consultant, I have found that the clients who best create cultures of ownership and accountability were usually the most productive and profitable. Conversely, the clients who did not usually were not. The two are connected.

Ownership and Accountability are Related, but Not the Same

Ownership, on its own, is the belief that *I own my results*.

Accountability, on its own, is the relationship of *being responsible to others for my results*.

They are related concepts, but not the same. I can own my results, but not feel responsible to or for others. Conversely, I can feel an overwhelming responsibility, but not own the results.

Creating Ownership and Accountability

I have noticed that some leaders are hesitant when they try to create cultures of ownership and accountability. Some become overly aggressive or demanding. Some feel like accountability is too much like confrontation or conflict. Others just are not sure what to focus on.

The Five Common Errors of Ownership and Accountability

1. **Not giving ownership:** Whether delegating a task to an individual or goals to a division, giving ownership includes giving decision-making authority and some kind of share in the risk/reward for performance. When this is lacking, people see the tasks and goals as *yours*, not *theirs*.

2. **Avoidance or neglect:** Many people in leadership just avoid dealing with issues. They may neglect to create the structures of ownership and accountability. For example, they do not set or clarify deadlines. They do not assign responsibilities. They do not clarify roles. They avoid conflict. They do not pounce on ambiguity and clear it up. They leave things undone.

3. **No follow-through:** Many leaders forget to follow-through. If they see things are off track, they do not move to bring them back. This is usually due to a lack of personal accountability on the part of the leader. Sometimes, it is due to a fear of confrontation with employees. It may be due to just not having the right habits and systems in place to keep track of what is going on. This creates incredible frustration and sometimes sets the leader up to lose respect in the eyes of those they lead.

4. **Micromanagement:** Many leaders try to lead through remote control. This usually is an expression of *perfectionism*, which is an expression of a *fear of failure*. These leaders do often do feel strong ownership and accountability. But, they do not know how to build it into others. In fact, they tend to believe that nobody cares as much as they do.

5. **Misaligned:** It is common for organizations to be misaligned in terms of a sense of purpose, priorities, and plans. This is usually accidental. For example, a division leader may be financially incentivized to keep operational costs low. Staff may be financially incentivized to improve performance.

However, if staff are successful in their performance, they'll be bonused more, and this will raise personnel (operational) costs, potentially causing the division leader to lose her incentive. Pursuing the success of the team now becomes a conflict of interest for the leader.

The Four Benefits of Ownership and Accountability

Improves Productivity and Efficiency

Ownership and accountability prevent workplace wandering from urgency to crisis and job creep. A good accountability system should serve staff by helping them stay focused on limited priorities.

Decreases Management Load

When employees feel ownership and accountability, they tend to self-manage more effectively. This allows their managers to focus more on more strategic questions.

Increases Personal Initiative

Employees who feel ownership and are provided with accountability tend to become even more motivated. They want to solve problems that they discover instead of waiting for someone else. They pay attention to what will benefit the company as a whole—not just their own department or team.

Improves Moral

Workplaces with a strong culture of ownership and accountability are motivating places to work. People are creative; they are doers; they are problem solvers. They get a share in the reward.

The Five Ingredients That Create Ownership

Shape the Person

The more skilled a person is, the higher their work ethic is, the more experience they have with a certain challenge or process—the easier it is for them to take ownership.

If you are leading people who have not yet developed the neccesary skills, work ethic, or experience, part of your role is to provide those opportunities.

This usually requires an intentional process of coaching and setting smaller, more achievable goals and providing appropriate levels of responsibility. The more ready someone is, the larger the goals and responsibility can be. Most people will grow with support even if given challenging goals.

Shape Outcomes

When people have an opportunity to give input or help determine the ultimate goal that is being pursued, they tend to own it.

The ability to shape outcomes is key to creating ownership. This does not mean that people should always get to choose their outcomes or even have the final say. But, when the people who are involved in achieving the outcomes are a part of shaping those outcomes, they often feel more ownership.

Shape the Means

By means, I am suggesting that employees work best when they can help answer the question, "How will this be done?" This works best when they know what the *edges of the sandbox* look like. These are the hard limits like budget, time, number of personnel, or anything else that might exist.

Employees who are able to shape the outcome and then given the ability to influence or decide how to achieve that outcome will perform more effectively.

Even in jobs where *how* something will be done is very prescribed, it is helpful if employees have an opportunity to provide feedback. The people on the front lines have a valuable perspective on what works and what does not.

Share Authority

To the degree that it is appropriate and possible, helping people and teams make good decisions for themselves makes everything else easier.

You can do this by ensuring that they have the necessary background knowledge and skills. You can also make it easier by having very clear organizational value and decision-making principles.

Organizations that define their values and how to apply them find that they provide guidance to everyone else. When priorities are clear, it is far easier for others to make decisions independently.

Share Risk and Rewards

Many of my early jobs allowed me to share the risk of poor performance, but not the reward of exemplary performance. It did not matter how well I did my job. I would not hear about it. If I heard anything, it was usually only if I was doing badly.

In some workplaces, there is a high toleration for low performers. This is dramatically demoralizing for others who will often feel like they have to pick up their slack.

People who feel recognized and valued for their contributions are more likely to keep contributing. They also become part of the process that shapes a culture of performance.

Four Ingredients for Accountability

The practice of accountability is largely about creating systems of measurement.

Define Performance Outcomes

Outcomes are well defined, and achievement is tied to clear metrics.

Behaviors

When you know what outcomes are desired, you can work to define the kinds of behaviors that will result in those outcomes.

This is similar to setting fitness goals. If my goal is to run a marathon, the behaviors (training regimen) will be different than if my goal is to deadlift 500 pounds.

First, define the desired outcome—then, define the behaviors needed to achieve that outcome.

Responsibility

When working with individuals, it should be clear that the individual is responsible. However, when working with teams, responsibility is often dissipated. This usually happens in one of two ways:

- Either *everyone* will be responsible. Which is the often same thing as no one will be responsible.
- One (or a few) people end up getting all the responsibility for everything.

To avoid this, make sure that each task has one (only one) person who is ultimately responsible that a task will be accomplished. Others may work on it. But one is responsible.

Also, keep track of who is carrying responsibilities and who is not. Make sure to readjust workloads if it looks like some people are not carrying their weight.

Timelines or Markers

Always define when something is due or when a report on progress will be made. For larger tasks or projects, define what partial progress would look like. Make your metrics as simple and as measurable as possible.

Is It Worth the Effort?

Leaders who want to shift to building a more engaged and accountable workforce often are confronted with the experience of feeling like it is not worth the effort. "It's faster just to do it myself." "It's easier if I just work with these three people I can trust."

In my experience, every single workplace that has taken the time to build ownership and establish systems of accountability has more than recouped their time and investment. None of them wonders if it is worth the effort. They all know the initial effort is what made everything else easier later.

CHAPTER 5

The Skills of Persuasion

People are generally better persuaded by the reasons which they have themselves discovered than by those which have come into the mind of others.

–Blaise Pascal

Skill #6: The Seven Critical Ingredients of Effective Executive Communication

The equation looks like this:

Effective communication = opportunities for better relationships = increased influence.

Leadership is about relationships. Relationships require communication. Communication builds your leadership.

What Does Effective Communication Sound Like?

Great leaders find ways to communicate effectively. Some may appear to be naturally articulate. But, that is deceptive.

I know a man who can command attention with his voice. At first. He has an amazing voice. A radio voice. He is also articulate and well spoken. You cannot help but expect him to say something profound.

But, he isn't profound. He does not even try to be. He is nice. His voice is nice to listen to. Conversations are friendly, but stay shallow. Even when the topics invite greater depth or substance. He is not doing anything wrong in this. It is not a failing. But, the result is: He has the tools most people think they should have to communicate. But, he does not have a message. As a result, he does not have much influence.

I know another man with cerebral palsy. When he speaks, he is very hard to understand. He has an interpreter who translates his English into everyone else's English.

He is loud. He seems disjointed. When I first met him, I felt awkward.

However, he speaks with intent and purpose. He is highly educated and has deep knowledge on his topic. He has a message.

As a result, he has influence. I have watched him shape the development of policy and law. He impacts the way other leaders think and act.

Having a great voice, being telegenic, knowing clever presentation tools...it can all help. But none of it is necessary. So, what is?

The Seven Essential Ingredients for Effective Executive Communication

One: Understand Your Audience

Understanding your audience includes knowing *who* your audience is and understanding *what* they are going through (where their minds and emotions are likely to be) when you address them.

I do a lot of public speaking. I have learned these lessons the hard way.

Years ago, I was asked to speak to a group of state commissioners. I was invited by a planner who had invited me to speak at an earlier conference. The talk had been popular. She invited me to speak again on the same topic to this different group. Which I did. But, I did not ask enough questions about the audience.

So, my talk flopped. They were dealing with completely different issues and could not use the information I gave them. Had I known (or picked up on this sooner during my presentation to them), I could have made adjustments to better serve them. But, I made assumptions about who they were and what they were interested in. I didn't adjust my topic to my audience.

Another time, I was asked to lead a day-long workshop with about 80 leaders. I had just come to the front to be introduced. As the host ended my introduction, she paused and then announced that a beloved colleague had just died. Then, she handed me the mic and walked off.

The audience looked at me, many of them with shock and emotion written on their faces. While I did not know this audience well, I had just learned some valuable information. I stopped my agenda, and we took a moment as a group to acknowledge what they had just learned. I do not recall what I said, but I acknowledged that this was unexpected and painful news for many. I let them know their colleague's passing was more important than the workshop. As a group, we briefly explored what they felt they needed to do to respond at this time. I also gave permission to anyone who felt like they needed to leave or move around to feel free if that helped.

I would have given that moment as much time as it needed. In reality, it took less than five minutes. But, they saw that I cared. They asked me to continue. I had their attention the rest of the day.

If I had just jumped into the workshop without acknowledging the news they had just received, the group probably would not have faulted me. (I was an outside guest.) But, they also would likely have been stuck on the emotion of the announcement. Instead, by acknowledging it and understanding what they needed, they were able to bracket their emotions, and I was able to provide what they wanted, which was to continue the workshop.

Understand and adjust to your audience. Don't make them adjust to you.

Two: Have a Clear Message

This seems obvious. But, we have all listened to a leader who rambled like an unprepared student responding to an essay question. They hope if they talk long enough, they will accidentally trip across the right things to say.

Even worse, we have listened to leaders who had no message and didn't care. They mistook having a podium for thinking that they, themselves, were so engaging that it did not matter what they did or said.

Last, there are situations, such as regularly scheduled meetings, presentations, or conferences (or articles or podcasts) where it starts to become more important to fill the time than actually present a message. I was recently invited as a guest on several podcasts, but the hosts were clearly not interested in a message (mine or their own). Instead, they were just filling a time slot.

Make sure you know what you want to communicate. Keep it relevant, simple, and focused. Anything else is frustrating and you will lose your audience.

Three: *Know What You Want to Accomplish*

It is not enough to have a message. You need to know what you are trying to accomplish. Not just in the big picture—but in that specific opportunity of communication.

What is that meeting supposed to accomplish?

That presentation?

That article?

That memo?

Be very clear on the outcome you are trying to produce. Then, craft your message to produce those outcomes.

Be vicious when it comes to pruning out anything else.

When I make mistakes in communication, it is usually because I have lost my own plot. I have forgotten what I needed or wanted to accomplish.

Correct that by getting clear about what you need to accomplish. Be ruthless about being on point.

Four: *Cultivate Healthy Confidence*

Healthy confidence requires four things: belief, ability, action, and humility.

If belief is lacking—you either will not act or will self-sabotage.

If ability is lacking—you are-self-deluded or a fraud.

If action is lacking—the confidence is a worthless sentiment.

If humility is lacking—you are self-serving.

All four need to be cultivated.

If you lack belief in your ability to communicate, build and practice your skills. Join Toastmasters. Hire a coach. The best way to build this skill is to find low-risk environments to practice and gain confidence.

If you lack ability, listen to feedback. Ask for input: "What is one thing I could do that would improve my presentations?" Turn your communication into experiments. Pick one area to improve and make a goal to practice that in the next few opportunities to communicate.

If action is lacking, create accountability. Set goals and communicate them to your team. Or hire a coach.

If humility is lacking, it is often difficult to self-diagnose. But your presentations will feel like they are about you—not your audience. So be preventative. Join a community of experienced, skilled, and confident communicators. Ask for feedback. They will not be as impressed with you as you are. Additionally, communicate in new mediums or to new audiences. But, they might be willing to help you grow.

Five: Be Clear and Concise

When people first speak publicly, the fear is usually, "I won't have enough to say!" Then, when handed a microphone, they cannot seem to stop talking. Yet, with all the words, it often remains difficult to know what they were trying to communicate. Saying too much, and being unclear about it, is the default for most people.

New executives sometimes talk too much because they do not know for sure what needs to be said. So, they say all of it in hopes of covering all their bases. Experienced executives can sometimes talk too much because no one will stop them, and they have fallen in love with their own voice.

The clearer you are on what you want to say and what you want, the easier it is to say less and communicate abundantly well. Both give you influence.

Speak less. Say more.

Six: Have a Call to Action

What should a listener or reader do with what you have said? Do not make them guess. Tell them.

I have a list of questions at the end of this section. They are calls to action. Questions that some readers will stop and answer for themselves. If I did not ask the question, they would not have anything to answer.

If you do not call people to action by either asking a clear question or providing a clear directive, people have nothing to respond to. Never hint or hope that people will figure out what you want them to do. Invite, tell, guide, instruct, ask—but be clear.

Putting it differently, if, as a leader, you are sharing information and have no need for it to generate action or changes in behavior, what is the value of the information? What are you trying to lead?

There are occasions where a call to action is not required. But, they are rare.

Leaders call people to action.

Seven: Communicate Frequently and Regularly

They say absence makes the heart grow fonder. But, most of the time, it just causes people to forget. Your communication needs to be frequent and regular. Then you can provide small, real-time reminders and encouragement. Do not save up your communication for when things are about to go off the rails. Or for the annual party.

When it comes to shaping culture and the performance ethic of your organization, you need to *frequently and regularly* reference these things. It is how you shape culture and expectations.

You cannot communicate vision only once—and then walk away. You cannot describe the value of a change once—and hope it sticks. You cannot have people read a policy once—and expect it will be fully complied with.

I have heard it said, "People leak. We have to keep filling them up." You are communicating enough when you see people moving their lips along with you. When they are making jokes about you repeating yourself. They should be able to hear your voice (hopefully saying helpful things!) in their head.

Lead with your words. They do not have to be a lot of words. But, they need to be there regularly.

Your Assignment

Think of the main messages you need to communicate over this week, month, or season of your organizational life. Take 15 to 20 minutes to think through the questions that I have asked here.

Communication cheat sheet

Understand your audience
- Who am I trying to communicate to?
- Are there different audiences within my organization who need me to tailor my communication to them?
- What is going on right now that might compete with my message? (Are there questions that need to be answered? Is there an issue or distraction that needs to be addressed?)
- What do they need or want right now?

Have a message
- What is it that I am trying to communicate?

Know what you want to accomplish
- What is the single most important outcome that I need to accomplish with this message?

Cultivate healthy confidence
- Which one of the following would I most benefit from growing in: belief, ability, action, or humility? What steps will I take to attain that growth?

Be clear and concise
- In one or two sentences, what is the key message I want to communicate?

Have a call to action?
- What response do I want from this audience?
- What is the simplest way to say or ask for this?

Communicate frequently and regularly
- What is the most important message that I need to communicate right now?
- How can I communicate this message more frequently? What different mediums of communication can I use? Are there different aspects of the message that I can focus on separately?

Answering these questions will help you communicate more clearly, with less effort, and achieve a greater response. If not, tell me about it.

Skill #7: How Savvy Leaders Engage High Performers without Being Pushy

I come back to motivation because, connecting to it well, is at the heart of effective leadership.

You cannot make an adult do something. You can only prevent (often at great expense) someone from acting.

Think about that.

No society, no workplace has a tool that can force ideal behavior. But, we do have prisons.

You Cannot Force Motivation

You can only force compliance. And that only works sometimes.

Here is how compliance-based leadership works:

1. Punish noncompliance. (You're-fired! Your pay is docked! You will never get that promotion! You are always going to get the lousy work around here!)
2. Reward compliance. (If you do A, we will give you B!)

Of course, most leaders do not think of themselves as a compliance-based leader. But, it is a go-to leadership approach.

Stick! Carrot!

Actually, it sounds more like:

- Let us set up an incentive program.
- We need to start writing people up. Let us create clear paper trails so that we can deal with some of these issues.
- Let us start Casual Fridays!
- We might need to think of a round of layoffs. To clear out the dead wood.

I am not suggesting that we do not reward employees or that we do not maintain performance or behavior standards. I absolutely believe in those things. It is just that those approaches *don't motivate.*

Why Do People Choose To Be Excellent? Why Would They Choose To Be Excellent with You?

Let us be candid here. One reason many people pursue leadership opportunities is that they are sick and tired of being on the receiving end of the stick-and-carrot approach.

But, that does not stop them from using it on others.

There are definitely reasons why:

- More people are pursuing entrepreneurship in today's economy.
- The gig economy is growing as well.
- Loyalty to an employer is decreasing as earning options increase.
- Potential employees decide they prefer one employer over another.

The Internet, like the printing press, steam engines, and assembly lines, has transformed how our economy works.

It has created options.

Options decrease the efficacy of external pressure (Stick! Carrot!) for your employees to stay with you and perform. This means leadership is even more important than ever. By that, I specifically mean the ability to inspire a shared sense of identity, vision, and purpose.

More Than Ever, Leaders Need to Engage the *Motivation* of Their Employees

The top 20 percent of your employees, the ones who tend to produce the highest results, are not motivated by the same things as the remaining 80 percent. Whereas the bottom 80 percent are more influenced by external motivators (the carrot and stick), the top 20 percent are driven by internal motivators.

I have spent a large part of my career in the nonprofit sector. One thing the nonprofit world usually does well is engage motivation. This is really their currency. They provide their staff, volunteers, and board an opportunity to connect to something. Something they feel is valuable.

What Specifically Motivates People?

There are a handful of unmysterious motivators in the workplace.

Specific motivators of employee performance and engagement have been extensively studied for over 100 years. In other words, despite the very common frustration supervisors feel, it is a well-understood topic.

Ranking varies a bit from study to study and over time. But, one study of over 200,000 employees at 50 different companies demonstrates typical results.[1] In order of ranking, the following were found to be motivators:

1. Camaraderie or quality of relationships with coworkers
2. Personal desire to do good work or self-respect
3. Recognition and encouragement from employer
4. A sense of purpose or impact
5. Personal and professional growth
6. Being able to meet the needs of others
7. Compensation
8. Positive management or leadership at company
9. Belief in company or product
10. Other

Compensation matters. But, once people no longer need to financially worry about basic financial security, other ends become more important. Those ends are often not expressed financially.

This does not mean you should start compensating people less. Or, that you should not have an incentive structure.

---

[1] 2014. The 7 Key Trends Impacting Today's Workplace. Available from: https://tinypulse.com/2014-employee-engagement-organizational-culture-report

What it means is that there are many more options for you to engage. Many of which will work better than compensation. Here are anecdotal examples of powerful non-monetary motivators that my clients have discovered:

- Recognizing and appreciating performance
- Public recognition or awards
- Regular employee get-togethers (lunches, social events, share-a-dish, etc.)
- Offering more time off or flexible schedules
- Offices in a nicer part of town
- Safer or more convenient parking
- Leadership coaching and training
- A "family" sense of culture
- Fun incentives (TVs, gadgets, experiences) were sometimes better incentives than straight cash, even if they were of a lower cash value.

There are many motivators for people. Compensation matters. But, not as much as you think.

A savvy leader will explore what actually motivates the people he or she leads.

How Will You Engage Motivation?

What are one or two actions you can take to better understand what motivates those you directly lead?

What are one or two ways that you can start to help them connect to what really motivates them?

PART III

Leading Your Leadership Team

CHAPTER 6

How to Lead Leaders

Stop Herding Cats. Start Working with Sheepdogs

How to Lead Leaders

When coaching leaders, one of the most common complaints I hear is, "I'm too busy."

That is not what they start out telling me. They initially say they want growth or they describe their vision. But there are obstacles. As we explore the obstacles something emerges that is taking up all their time and energy. It is preventing them from achieving their vision. It often steals their joy. Frequently it impacts their health or relationships.

When I suggest they work on that and change the dynamic, they often insist that they are too busy to learn to become less busy. This exposes that they are choosing to be too busy. Because being busy feeds something in them.

When someone will not stop doing something that they say makes them miserable or prevents them from hitting their goals...well...they are getting something out of it.

What Being Too Busy Does for Us

Maybe being so busy:

- Squeezes our adrenal gland. Sweet, sweet adrenaline.
- Makes us feel important. Because important people have lots to do.
- Reinforces the image that we are, in fact, the only smart person in the room.
- Allows us to avoid something. Or someone.
- Excuses our lack of direction or decisiveness.

Here is the deal: Whatever level of complexity you lead or manage, there is someone else who is not as smart as you who is effectively handling more. And, getting better results.

On top of it all, that someone else also has a full life. They make it to their kid's soccer games. They have date nights with their spouse. They take vacations. They are focused, experiencing success, and happy with life.

What kind of magic is this?

They probably were not gifted with a mature team of brilliant and experienced people. Nor did they inherit an organization that runs like a top, where everyone naturally loves each other and makes crazy money hand over fist without trying.

They simply do not want to be busy. There is nothing in them that is being fed by being busy. They recognize that being busy is costly. So, they find a way to accomplish goals without doing it all themselves.

They might like to work. They may prefer to stay active. They might, in fact, keep themselves busy.

But they are not *too* busy.

What Being Too Busy Costs Us

Being too busy is costly. This list is not definitive. But, here is how I see my clients paying for being too busy:

- High personal stress
- Missed opportunities
- Poor health
- Unable to provide strategic leadership
- Unable to take a break and regain energy and perspective
- Loss in overall business value (due to making too many functions dependent on the executive)
- Strained team relationships
- Strained or neglected family relationships
- High staff turnover
- Drama and conflict

- Difficulty building and retaining a high-performing management team
- Poor follow-through or inconsistent completion of goals
- Tendency for self-medication: alcohol, eating poorly, and so on

I could go on. But, you get the point.

What you also may have noticed is that many of the consequences of being too busy are situations that create more work.

Being too busy just makes you busier.

Here Is What You Are Doing and How to Stop

Identify What Being Busy Feeds in You

What are you getting out of this? This is an important enough question to spend time reflecting on.

For some people, the answer is pretty clear. For others, it is either difficult to see or difficult to accept.

Ask your friends. Ask your coworkers. Ask a coach or counselor.

Think through the 3Ss. Are you pursuing significance? I could not tell you how many leaders brag to me about their 80-hour work weeks. Or how they are the only person in their organization the big clients can talk to. Or how no one else in their company has their eye for quality. All are dynamics that undermine organizational performance.

Are you trying to create security? Are you afraid that if you stop working, everything will fall apart? Or that you will not be seen as valuable or needed if you do not put in the extra time? Or you are struggling with a sense of scarcity and are afraid that if you stop working there will not be enough?

Are you finding (or hoping for) some satisfaction in this? Some people use work or being busy to hide from other issues in life. Some people have found a kind of unhealthy equilibrium in being too busy. It is like meeting someone who is only happy in a relationship if there is drama. It is not that they like the drama, but the things that lead to drama just seem to *feel right.* Or maybe you love the work you are currently doing and you are afraid you won't enjoy stepping into greater leadership.

Many of these desires are health and appropriate. It is healthy to provide value and feel a sense of worth and significant. It's important to have security. Finding satisfaction is meaningful.

However, do not attempt to pursue healthy things in unhealthy ways. Being too busy is like that. Once you have discovered what is driving you, you can find better ways to meet those needs.

Ways that are more meaningful. Ways that are more effective. Less costly.

Develop Your Big Picture

What are you trying to accomplish? What is your organization trying to accomplish?

Here is what I have found. Leaders who are too busy often fall into two different camps:

1. **Frustrated Visionaries:** They know what they want to accomplish, but other priorities keep emerging to interrupt them. These other priorities are driving their decisions and actions—not their vision.
2. **Self-Made Sisyphus:** Sisyphus was a Greek king who Zeus decided to punish. He was forced to endlessly roll a boulder up a hill only to have it roll back down when he got to the top. These leaders are often unclear about what they are trying to accomplish. But they stay busy hoping they will eventually figure out their *why.* Or they confuse the work and the effort with the outcomes they hope to produce.

So again, getting honest about what really drives you will help you understand and manage your priorities.

Clarifying your big priorities helps you visualize the big picture. This, in turn, helps you (and others) focus.

When other people can see what the big picture is, especially if they were a part of creating it, they can and usually will work to support it (when allowed).

I know…you may feel too busy to take time to think about where you are trying to go. But what is the point of all your effort?

Too many leaders focus more on being busy than on productivity.

Busy people are often not the most productive. It is not true that everything would fall apart if you intentionally set a specific ball or a plate down for a moment to figure out, "Where are we going anyway?" and "Why?"

Because you will. Eventually, everyone drops the balls they are juggling. They stop keeping their plates spinning. We get sick, a crisis pops up, something falls apart…and they drop something.

The world keeps spinning just fine without us.

Being too Busy Is Very Much a State of Mind

Being too busy has more to do with mindset than the demands that are placed on you. Ignoring the consequences of being too busy is similarly a state of mind.

I routinely work with clients who is hope to scale up and build a larger organization. They usually start out (or soon hits a point) where they are "too busy." In every single situation, when we figure out how get them to do focused, productive work on the right things—their organization is both able to grow and they find that they are suddenly less busy.

That is why, turning things around has so much to do with addressing how you see yourself in the context of your life. Here is the really cool thing: Learning to be (and enjoy being) accomplished *without* needing to be so busy allows you (and others) to experience a deeper, richer, more enjoyable you.

You grow as a result of this. Everyone else gets the benefit of that.

That is worth it on its own.

Get Ruthless about Clarity

Once you know your big picture (whether for the next five years or five months), get clear about a few things. This might feel like work. But, what it does is it makes everything else so much easier.

When there are clear roles and responsibilities, clear targets, clear ways to measure progress, and clear indicators of success, the following happens:

- People begin to self-manage.
- You stop herding cats, chickens, and turtles and start working with sheepdogs.
- People get along better.
- Team meetings become far more focused and productive.
- Problems are caught far earlier.
- Opportunities are taken.
- Creativity and innovation begin to reemerge.
- Quality improves.
- Productivity improves.

That feels like magic. But, you know you put the hard work in the right place. The leaders who accomplish a lot without increasing their effort focus their time in only three areas:

1. **Defining direction**: Discussed earlier. Setting direction and sorting through priorities.
2. **Finding, building, and guiding people:** High-performing leaders help others do a lot. They do not do it themselves.
3. **Gathering resources**: Make sure everyone has the resources they need to succeed.

Keep it simple. Get more done.

Face Your Ego and Your Fears

Leaders everywhere struggle with what is often called "The Imposter Syndrome." It is not discussed openly. But, it is common.

Common like dirt.

Leaders, particularly owners and executives, frequently struggle with ego and fear. Ego and fear hijack our priorities and commandeer how we use our time. People might suspect ego, but most would be surprised to know how common it is for an executive to feel fear.

Learning to recognize when *ego* or *fear* begins to inform a decision or a priority is a major step to cultivating leadership self-awareness.

Simply put, "The Imposter Syndrome" is the idea that if others really knew us, they would know that we are not enough. Or that we made mistakes. We are not knowledgeable, able, skilled, self-controlled, motivated...good...enough for our role.

So, we work hard to prove them wrong. Or, keep them from finding out.

Here are proven approaches to address ego and fear:

- **Practice gratitude:** I bring this up a lot. Because it changes people. Gratitude requires two things: The ability to see good outside of ourselves and the humility to recognize that someone or something else was responsible for that good. Gratitude directly confronts both ego and fear.
- **Reframe success:** Learn to see and value progress—not perfection. Focus on being better than you were—not better than someone else.
- **Recognize offenses, worry, or fear:** When someone bruises your ego or something happens that triggers anxious thoughts, recognize it. Name it. See it for what it is. A very normal, human response. Acknowledge it. Deal with it if that makes sense. But, it does not need to own you. Do not let it.
- **Visualize obstacles and plan for them:** The best athletes and coaches visualize the obstacles as much as the victory. They expect to encounter one on the path to the other. They get clear about the challenges. Then get to work imagining or creating innovative solutions for the problem. Then they take action.
- **Learn:** Being teachable challenges ego. Learning builds confidence. Leaders or organizations who aren't teachable tend to repeat their mistakes or stop taking risks. Ask yourself these questions whenever you either accomplish something or meet a challenge:
  - What just happened?
  - What did I (or my team) do to make this happen?

- º What can I (we) learn from this?
- º What will I (we) do the next time?

Six Habits of the Best Team Leaders

Leaders are in the business of leading. You will often find them leading teams. Seems obvious.

This seems so obvious that most people get it wrong. They believe *leading* means receiving a promotion into management. They believe that *team* is any group of people sharing proximity at work.

I have found that the most commonly utilized team building process is:

- Bring a group of people together.
- Use the word *team* a lot when you talk to them.

Written that way, you can probably see that this might not work. But not for lack of people trying.

Most teams underperform. Actually, worse than underperforming, they might cost the organization time and money. They often pull others off-purpose. They frequently absorb attention and energy.

This is not to say they are not hard workers or are not staying busy. They often are very busy, working hard. But, they are not producing at the level they could or should. And, they are putting in too much effort along the way.

The Team Matters. The Leader Matters More. But, Only If the Leader Builds a Unified Team

Leaders often stress about getting the right team members. "Get the right people on the bus," is language that Jim Collins popularized. He is right. The right people matter.

But, less than perfect people can accomplish great things if the team is led well to function well over a sustained time. And, it is *always* and *only* leadership that makes that happen.

Studies conducted by Google[1] and at Harvard[2] demonstrated that *how* a team functions is a better predictor of performance than *who* is on it.

How a team functions is shaped and maintained by a leader.

For Senior Leaders, Look Less for Technical Skills and More for People Skills

By people skills, I do not mean they are chatty or nice or fun to be around.

I mean they know how to engage well with high performers and low performers. They know how to manage meetings and conversations. They are willing to hold others to account and be held to account. They effectively wade into difficult conversations and get them on track. Most importantly, they create a sense of safety and trust in the team.

Technical skills matter. But, senior leaders rarely do the technical work. They should be focused on leading. More specifically, helping their team perform to its potential.

When you look for senior leaders, look for people who have demonstrated an ability to unite and orient a group of people around a common purpose and goal and then successfully led them to completion.

Watch for they do; it is easier than you might think. The following are the principles or practices that will be demonstrated by anyone ready for effective service as a senior leader.

How Great Leaders Build Unity, Alignment, and High-Performing Teams

1. **They Prioritize Quality Communication**
   - They communicate frequently but stay focused and purposeful.
   - They ask and encourage good questions.
   - They provide information in a timely and complete way.

---

[1] Rework.withgoogle.com.2020.https://rework.withgoogle.com/print/guides/5721312655835136/ (accessed June 26, 2020).
[2] Edmondson, Amy C. 2018. *The Fearless Organization: Creating Psychological Safety in the Workplace for Learning, Innovation, and Growth.* John Wiley & Sons.

- They test assumptions.
- They encourage and support face-to-face time.
- They take sufficient time to understand/explore resistance, pressure, or lack of movement from others.

2. **They Articulate and Develop Common Values/Principles**
- They ensure that everyone understands the basic ground rules that everyone needs to create a culture that is both respectful and productive.
- They articulate the underlying values that guide decision-making and behavior.
- They work to appropriately enforce these values and principles when violated.

3. **They Comfortably Define and Ensure Understanding of Purpose and Expectations**
- They identify a clear, concise, and common purpose for everything: What is the purpose of this meeting? What is the goal of this team? What is the theme for this year? Good leaders know. Great leaders make sure their team knows.
- They make sure everyone understands their role and the roles of others on the team.
- They clarify the desired outcomes and expectations for each position and the team.
- The clarify individual and joint responsibilities and timelines.
- They clarify how these outcomes and responsibilities contribute to the success of others and the purposes of the organization.

4. **They Create Mutual Beneficiality**
- They work to ensure that everyone feels that they are benefiting from the work relationship.
- They take the time to engage an individual's enlightened self-interest. In other words, shepherding alignment between underlying personal interests and the interests of the team or organization.

5. **They Ask for and Provide Timely Follow-Through on Agreed Actions**
- They personally follow through on whatever is agreed.

- They create accountability and offer support so that others do as well.
- They communicate as soon as possible and clearly when follow-through or timeliness will not be achieved so that others can adjust or prepare.

6. **They Make It Safe for Mutual Accountability**
   - They create a workplace dynamic where people have a voice and a mutually understood process to follow for grievances, renegotiating terms, requesting changes, and holding each other to account.
   - They actively hold others to account for workplace behavior, performance, and outcomes.
   - They understand how and why to use structure in the accountability process. Structure where everyone can discuss what is working well, what is being learned, expectations can be clarified (if needed), and improvements can be made. These can be incorporated into regular meetings or scheduled in intervals.

Most of the behaviors in this list should be able to be observed in a single, normal (but well-run) staff meeting.

Additionally, it is a useful list for evaluating and guiding your own habits when you engage with your staff.

Try it. When planning your next meeting, sit down with this list and take five minutes to decide how you will bring each of these six ingredients into the meeting.

Try it with a project. Try it with the whole organization.

How to be a Superb Leader without Being an Expert

There is a sobering maxim, called the *Peter Principle* [3] that says, "Managers rise to the level of their incompetence." This principle can be observed in nearly every organization.

---

[3] Peter, L.J., and R. Hull. 1969. *The Peter Principle.* Morrow.

Someone who had great (or at least adequate) performance in their role gets promoted. They are successful in this new role. They get promoted again.

This continues until they rise to a level where they no longer perform well. It looks like this:

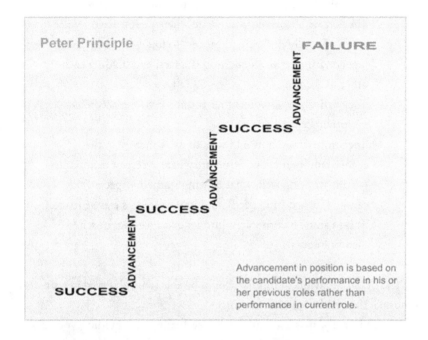

However, sometimes this plays out a little differently, especially in fast growth organizations or divisions. Sometimes, instead of a leader being formally promoted, organizational growth beneath the leader translates into their responsibilities growing or changing. Up until the point where they are no longer in their "sweet spot" of effectiveness.

When this happens, it can unfortunately look or feel like the leader is failing. The word *failure* connotes somebody crashing and burning. More often, leaders, especially senior leaders, do not fail spectacularly. Instead, they hit their ceiling. They stagnate. They get in their own way.

They are no longer able to produce new success. Because moving back to a role where they can be successful is often viewed as a demotion—they focus on survival as opposed to results. There is a tendency to redefine success as maintaining and holding onto the status quo.

They are no longer able to provide lift or growth to the organization. So, they do not try.

They may even prevent others from producing that lift or growth. It may be due to jealousy. It might be due to the fear of others discovering that their job could be done at a higher level.

This leader does not need to be a victim of the Peter Principle. But, they do need to change how they view success.

There are many reasons, or thinking errors, that cause someone to hit this ceiling. Two are common and related. Both revolve around an unhealthy relationship with *expertise:*

Thinking Error 1: "I Need to Be the Expert at Anything I Am Involved In"

This could be because of insecurity or pride. Many arrogant people are also insecure. So, perhaps those are two sides of the same coin.

Either way, it is a significant problem when a leader believes that he or she needs to be the smartest person in every room. If this is their thinking error, they will demonstrate one or more of the following behaviors:

- A rigid and self-deluded reality where they believe because they are an expert in area "A," they are also an expert in area "B." For example, the brilliant engineer who also believes he or she understands executive leadership or business development.
- Avoiding rooms where they may not be the smartest person. Refusing to join true peer groups or intentionally pursue personal development. Preferring to lead everything they are involved with or surround themselves with people who need their expertise.
- Pushing the actual smartest person(s) out of the room they are in. This often looks like finding faults with or petty reasons to dismiss the value of the other individual. A leader with this thinking error will often dismiss, diminish, or seek to contain or remove the person perceived to be the *smarter* person. If

the *smarter* person has any sense of self-worth, he or she will
go elsewhere.

This results in organizations where everyone learns not to shine too
brightly, and dull people thrive.

Surprisingly, this is very common in fields that consists of experts: IT,
law, medicine, engineering, behavioral or mental health, religious institu-
tions, and so on. Self-made men and women often show this trait. They
needed to do everything to get to where they are. They have achieved
expertise and success. Do not suggest that they should rely on or trust
someone else.

While the description above may seem like we are talking about someone who appears to be very arrogant or brash, it may not always manifest
that way.

To the contrary, this attitude can sometimes appear very humble and
self-effacing. The world is full of small business owners who should run
medium or large businesses, but are unwilling or unable to step out of
their comfort zone of expertise. They may chalk this up to being content
where they are, accepting their limits, or not overreaching. All of which
can be fine. But not when motivated from a place of, "*I'm* as good as *we*
will ever get." This mindset is not limited to small businesses. It applies to
any size of organization or industry.

Thinking Error 2: "I am Not the Expert, So I Do not Get Involved"

This can come from actual deference to the experts. But, it can also stem
from insecurity. Either way, it is negligent for a leader to *not get involved*
or *leave it to the experts.*

Governing boards (all kinds) frequently demonstrate this willingness
to be negligent. Of course, it is not framed as negligence. Instead, it is
framed as, "Our leader/people/team is amazing! We trust them completely!" Due diligence is set aside.

Senior leaders often make this mistake as well. A CFO may say, "I'm
the numbers woman. I don't need to understand the needs of our customers." The VP of HR may say, "I deal with recruitment, training, and

compliance. I'm up to my eyeballs in workshops. I don't have time to understand strategy."

How to Be Superb without Being an Expert

A number of years ago, I worked with a nonprofit that employed several hundred people and are a significant regional social services provider. I was helping them with leadership development and strategy.

I noticed that their IT director attended all my workshops and planning sessions. Curious about it, I asked. He explained that understanding the actual mission, needs, desires, and frustration of all the other department leaders helped him understand how to better serve them through his department. *Even though we were not discussing IT needs.*

This guy got it. He was taking the time to learn just enough. He was comfortable leaving his actual expertise at the door (no one asked him to) and being a learner and asking questions. He was oriented toward everyone else's success. He understood that his department only really shined if he was able to help everyone else shine.

To Excel at Senior Leadership, Learn To Do These Three Things

A. Learn to Know *Just Enough*

Learn just enough technical literacy to understand what others are saying. *Just enough* proficiency to discuss performance. *Just enough* to know when questions need to be asked. *Just enough* is enough. Become comfortable with *just enough.*

B. Learn to be Comfortable Being the Dummy *or* Become an Expert at Asking the Right Questions

I get hired because of my expertise. But, I earn my living by being the dummy.

I do not know very much about a lot of things. But, I am really good at asking the right questions. I don't need to know the answers. I just have to know enough be able to pull the answers out of others. That takes being willing to ask questions. It is the same for excellent leaders.

Here is a little secret I have learned from years of work in boardrooms and executive offices: Most of these people are highly intelligent and well educated. They also regularly run up against the limits of their expertise. But, most are afraid to ask questions. So, they often fake expertise. Which means they do not grow.

Do not fake it. Ask the questions.

C. Facilitate Everyone Else's Success

Great leaders realize that their expertise is often irrelevant to their role as leader. They can achieve greater and more sustained success by getting more from the expertise of others. So, they learn how to do that.

At the senior level, the best leaders focus nearly all their energy on surrounding themselves with very competent people. These leaders help their people to shine very brightly. Then they focus the collective brilliance of their people in the same direction.

Do you want to avoid creating *Peter Principle* situations? To avoid placing them in a position where they will not succeed, look for:

Someone who *does not* demonstrate the thinking errors described earlier: needing to be an expert or leaving everything to the experts.

Someone who can learn just enough, is willing to be a dummy, and able to understand that a leader's job is to facilitate the success of others.

Someone who can succeed in the new role—not someone who was successful in an old role.

CHAPTER 7

Make It or Break It Executive Leadership Practices

Leadership that matters is entirely found in choices, actions and results.

Active Leadership

Early in my consulting career, I was asked to meet pro bono, with a nonprofit executive, some supporters, and his board. This nonprofit had a long history of providing a very unique and needed service to the community. They were set up for easy success. But, they were struggling.

We met for a couple of hours. I listened to their updates. I asked a few questions. Two issues became quickly clear:

- The executive director, who was the founder, didn't want to lead. He was passionate about their mission. But he did not like and would not do the work of leadership. Despite not wanting to lead, he did not want to give up his leadership position.
- As is true for most non profit boards, their board was not a functioning board. They were nice people. They were committed to the mission. But, they were not providing governance. Out of a sense of *like* for the executive director, and perhaps his position as founder, they enabled his passivity. They were not leading. They were not ensuring that leadership existed.

There were no active leaders. It was an unhealthy organization. It no longer exists today. Which is too bad because the service they provided was so valuable.

I offered my services for free if the executive director was willing to accomplish a couple of simple, basic tasks. I would even help him with those tasks. These tasks typically take, at most, a couple of hours to complete.

"That's what the other consultants told me," he said.

Other consultants?

I had run into someone who was looking for a Fairy Godmother who would make all his leadership work go away.

No thanks.

What Active Leaders Are and Why No One Else Is Acceptable

Active leaders do the work of leadership. It is about as simple as that.

Despite the simplicity, there are leadership positions all over the place filled by passive, half-hearted, sluggish, avoidant, or lazy people. They may have aspired to the position, *but not to the work of leadership.*

Active leaders lead. They actively look ahead to set goals and identify opportunities and challenges. They engage with the present to ensure standards of performance, and the needs of those they lead and serve are being met. They review the past to track progress and learn, constantly improving their teams.

Active leaders:

- Make informed decisions
- Ensure accountability and follow-through
- Take care of people—both those they lead and their customers
- Take care of their mission—they ensure progress and success
- Invest in their personal development and growth
- Start, initiate, and change
- End projects, initiatives, or relationships that need to be ended

Active leadership is not an end-all trait. Some leaders are very active, but their drive and motivation come from unhealthy and unhelpful sources such as fear, pride, a desire to control, a sense of not being enough, or the need to win at any cost.

But, if a leader is not active, they are a leader in name only.

Active Leadership and Senior Leadership

Senior leaders should be active leaders. Never select someone for senior leadership if they do not actively lead. Leadership is not an award. It is not a way to recognize longevity or loyalty. It is a role and responsibility.

Senior leaders need to lead actively. They are people you will rely on. They are there to lift the load. Not be one more person to manage.

Select for this trait.

How Organizations Squelch Active Leadership

Some organizations struggle to attract or retain active leaders. They often blame the market. Or, "Kids these days." The reality is that great leaders are out there, but they can pick and choose where they go. What would make them choose you?

Five common ways organizations discourage active leadership:

1. **Creating a personality-driven leadership culture**. Some strong executives use their strength to consolidate authority and control decision-making. This may express itself through micromanagement, undercutting other's decisions, or otherwise limiting the leadership of others. It may also express itself through a brilliant, charismatic leader who is always swooping in to rescue others. This demotivates and *deactivates* other leaders. It tends to attract people who prefer to work in an environment where their decision-making responsibility is limited. It tends to push away naturally active leaders who recognize they cannot thrive in this environment.
2. **Withholding decision-making authority**. Some executives discourage or don't allow their leaders to make real decisions. They do not effectively delegate their authority. They do not delegate enough

information or resources and decision-making ability. They require that they be consulted too often over too many decisions.

3. **Ambiguous decision-making authority**. Some leaders let people make decisions but are never clear about what is *over the line*. Anyone's decision might be undercut. For any reason. In this context, most people stop being active, and the best will usually leave.

4. **Withholding information:** Some leaders divide and segment knowledge. Sometimes this is intentional. Sometimes, it is an accidental by-product of poorly designed systems or communication. Either way, most people with insufficient information will not act. Those who do often find they are making mistakes and become cautious.

5. **Not matching skills with responsibilities**. One of the most common reasons I see for inactive leadership is a leader who just does not know how to do their job. They were not selected based on ability. Either support is not available to help them increase their ability or they are uncomfortable requesting it or they just don't have the interest or aptitude to learn this role.

How Organizations Cultivate Active Leadership

An organization can encourage active leadership (and dramatically improve performance) by:

- **Selecting for active leaders—addressing inactive leaders**.
  The example from the top speaks more than any leadership training program could hope to. Choose active leaders. Hold inactive leaders accountable.
- **Creating clarity in roles, responsibilities, and decision-making authority**. Many people do not act because they just do not know the boundaries of their *sandbox*. So, they act like employees waiting for the next steps to be dictated to them. The time you spend creating clarity will be more than multiplied back to you through leaders who can solve problems and take advantage of opportunities in real time.

- **Effective communication**. Making sure that the quality of information and methods of communication are used to support and empower your people.
- **Cultivating a tolerance for error**. Error is not ideal. But, it is inevitable. Use it as an opportunity for growth. High-performing organizations accept that errors happen and have processes for addressing it. This allows it to be addressed quickly and early—mitigating damage. It allows people to learn and grow from it—mitigating repeated mistakes.

Managing to Outcomes

The Questions That Need to Be Answered

I have three kids, ages seven, six, and three. My wife and I both own our own businesses. We are busy. Any morning offers the opportunity for getting swept into whitewater rapids of demands, needs, chores, disputes, tears, feeding, changing...and then I go to work. Open my e-mails, and I could be swept over the waterfall of requests, meetings, updates, changes, proposals, answers, interventions, calls...and then, I go home and am swept away again.

It is easy, perhaps the easiest thing, to just click into survival mode. Do what needs to be done. Take care of what is right in front of me. Deal with the closest, most important crisis of the moment. Just try to make it to the end of the day without major damage.

But this is just thrashing around. Trying to solve problems by working harder.

What happens, understandably, is I can easily forget (or perhaps never even consider) what am I trying to build. What am I trying to create in terms of my marriage? My family? My business?

What will success look like? At work? At home? In my life? In my clients' lives?

What am I trying to accomplish?

Most leaders, the majority, in fact, become very skilled at navigating situations and storms. We become captains who can handle any stormy sea.

We just are not sure what port we are trying to get to or why.

Question One: What Are We Trying to Accomplish?

Begin with the end in mind.

—Stephen Covey

This quote is the second of *The 7 Habits of Highly Effective People* described by Stephen Covey.

It is another way of describing outcome-focused leadership and management.

Practicing this habit is one of the easiest ways to dramatically increase your productivity and impact. It is one of the most effective ways to increase your team's performance. An ideal leader will always ask the following kinds of questions:

- What is our focus?
- What is our purpose?
- What is success (and how will it be measured or recognized)?

The reason for these questions is targeting. Selecting a destination.

There is no exception to this—outstanding leaders know what they are trying to accomplish. Any leader who cannot describe what they are trying to accomplish, in the big picture, is operating below their capacity.

It is easy to avoid answering the big picture question. You just talk about all the small picture things that need to get done.

That is why senior leaders need to make the big picture a habit. It is also why, when building a high-performing leadership team, we need to screen for people who make this a habit.

All senior leaders should think this way. It should be a requirement in the selection process. Otherwise, you are not hiring a leader. Leaders, by definition, are going somewhere—on purpose.

Effective leaders build a culture that insists on asking the question and creating answers.

It is leadership to define the answer to this question, both at the macro level of "What is our focus or purpose as a company?" and at the micro level of "What is this new project/policy/ position supposed to accomplish?"

When teams and employees know what they are supposed to accomplish, they can more easily self-manage.

Question Two: How Will We Know if We Succeed?

If you can't measure it, you can't manage it.

—Peter Drucker

Successful leaders define the metrics for success before the fact. Everyone else will define the metrics of success after the fact. Think about that.

Leaders and leadership teams who achieve the most start out knowing how they will measure progress and accomplishment. They have such a clear vision of what they are trying to build, it is easy to describe measurements around it.

They ask questions such as:

- What will indicate that we have been successful?
- What will be different or changed or new or gone, and how can we measure it?
- How will things improve as a result of success?

Unsuccessful leaders resist asking those questions upfront. They prefer to do a lot of work, splash a lot in the pool, and based on how tired they feel, call it a good swim. They are not interested in defining laps, speed, distance, or calories burned.

I am oversimplifying. But, only a little. As I have mentioned, it is very, very common for a proud leader to brag to me about his 60-, 70-, or 80-hour workweeks.

The fastest way to burst that bubble is to ask what he was trying to accomplish and if he got it done.

Question Three: What Makes This Accomplishment Important?

Why should anyone care?

— Simon Sinek

I have learned the incredible value of clarifying, "Why are we doing this?" with clients. It taps into their motivation. Which is important.

My standard contract usually takes at least a few months of engagement with a client. Over time, a client's urgencies shift. Priorities fade in their focus. New demands or challenges or opportunities emerge. The client's attention and energy wander.

Because I know their answer to *Why?* (Because I asked them before they even hired me), I can go back and ask, "Does this still matter?" It usually does.

So, I can help them determine if it still matters more than the new project, demand, or shiny object that caught their attention. It usually does.

So, I can help them get back on track. They usually do. Then, they accomplish the goal. And, they become high performers.

Good leaders flesh out and remind themselves and others the answer to the question, *Why?*

They might frame it differently:

- What if this fails or you did nothing? What would be the impact?
- What difference will success make for (fill in the blanks)?
- What does it currently cost you (or what are you not experiencing) because you have not yet succeeded in this area?
- Who will success matter the most to and how will it impact them?

How to Apply This Toward Building Your Dream Team

1. Practice outcome-focused leadership and management yourself
   - This will help you understand it so that you can teach and coach it.

- By practicing it, you will attract the kind of people who think this way to your team.

2. **Build your team to be outcome-focused**
   - Recruit and screen for this quality in anyone who you bring into senior leadership; it should be a required trait and capacity.
   - Model this practice. Make it part of your culture.
   - Coach your managers and leaders to think in terms of outcomes. Do not assume that they will naturally understand it or have developed the habits of being outcome-focused.

3. **Build outcome-focused approaches into your culture and structure**
   - Planning should be outcome-focused.
   - Policy development should be outcome-focused.
   - Hiring decisions and practices should be outcome-focused.
   - Incorporate the following simple questions into all your practices: "What is this supposed to accomplish?" "How will we know if we succeeded?" "Why does it matter?"

Easily Managed Priorities

What is the one thing, that by so doing, makes everything else easier or unnecessary?

—Gary Keller

A few years ago, I started practicing Brazilian Jiu-Jitsu (BJJ). I love it. The workouts are fast, furious, and sweaty.

Because I am a strength and conditioning instructor and train regularly, I had a definite size and strength advantage over many of my classmates and even most of the instructors. Unfortunately, BJJ was developed so that smaller, weaker people could out-grapple and force bigger, stronger opponents to tap out or *submit*.

As I write this, I am still a white belt, a novice. In the BJJ system, it usually takes years to progress to the next belt. New white belts are known for thrashing around a lot without accomplishing much.

New white belts who are also strong and fit are the most famous for this. For my first year of training, I put enormous effort into accomplishing very little. In fact, the development of my technique suffered because of my tendency to try to muscle through.

This resulted in slower progress and a long list of self-inflicted injuries. It is informative to me that so many smaller and not as strong classmates have surpassed me in progress. It was only when I learned to stop thrashing and trying to power through movements that I started to really grow.

Advancement to the next belt comes, in part, when I learn to stop unnecessary movement. To only move in ways that should produce my intended result. No additional effort. No thrashing around.

I have noticed something about my instructors: They never work as hard as I do. They never get as tired as I do. They never seem as sweaty.

They always know what their last move was, where they are at right now, and what they are going to do next.

During my first year, while squishing me into the mat or tying me into a pretzel, they made helpful observations like, "You are working too hard."

Yes, I was.

It took me a long time to accept that there was little connection between how hard I worked and getting submitted less.

The Divide

When working with successful, senior leaders, a clear divide emerges in terms of productivity, lifestyle, and work habits. One either side of this divide are two kinds of leaders.

Effort-Focused Leaders

There are leaders who work very hard. They put in long hours. They feel constantly busy, often putting out fires or dealing with emergencies. They are often rushed and stressed. There is never enough time to get caught up. Truth be told, they often love the adrenaline of it all.

Effort is equated to success. They say things like (this is a direct quote), "I'm cutting back at work; now I'm only putting in 80 hours." Some came up in industries that associated the number of hours billed with leadership productivity. Others were raised with a work ethic where pats on the back were only given to people who were constantly busy.

Priority-Focused Leaders

Then there are leaders who work precisely. They do not equate the number of hours worked with productivity. They easily leverage resources around them so they do not need to work as hard. They seem to have time. Not spend time. This does not mean they do not work hard, but it means they do not confuse being busy with producing results.

Results are equated to success. Because of this, they focus tightly on accomplishing those results. In fact, they experience the freedom that comes with accomplishing more while doing less work.

Only Priority-Focused Leadership will Produce More with Less Effort

Leaders who develop clear and simple priorities for themselves, their team, and their organization will win every time. They are the *upper belts* of the leadership world.

Everyone else is working too hard.

Despite however much an effort-focused leader might accomplish, their effort:results ratio is off. They could accomplish far more. Or work far less. Or both. It would be their choice. But, until they change their perspective, they are not free to make it.

After years of executive coaching, I have learned that the effort-focused leader will nearly always push back against my assertion that they are working too hard. They resist it.

I get that.

It is like BJJ. When I was first learning, and I felt someone maneuver for a choke, it was the most natural thing to work harder to get free.

So, I thrashed. And wore myself out or made a mistake. And got choked anyway.

But I am learning. I do not work nearly as hard now and I get choked far less often.

What Is a Priority?

If you chase two rabbits, you will lose them both.

—Origin unknown

The English word *priority* emerged in the fourteenth century. For the next 500 years, it was primarily used as singular noun. The first thing. The one thing. The most important thing.

It has only been since the 1950s that the word has morphed into the more common plural: *priorities.*

To keep up with these new priorities, we have developed new concepts, such as multitasking, which numerous studies have shown to impair overall performance to a degree similar to sleep deprivation or alcohol use.

In fact, we know the fastest way to work through a list of priorities is to focus on one priority at a time, until completion. Then move on to the next. The leader who learns this habit will be far more productive than the leader attempting to focus on everything—and therefore, nothing.

Despite this knowledge, leaders still attempt to multitask their way through long lists of priorities.

Yes, there are some jobs and times when it is necessary to manage broadly. And, all effective leaders learn to watch multiple indicators at once. But, when leaders do not know what the single most important priority is for themselves and their team, they tend to end up thrashing.

What Priority-Focused Leaders Do That Is Different

When selecting senior leaders, effort-based leaders often look like obvious choices. They work hard, they are determined, and they are not afraid to lean into it. They stand out against everyone else who does not seem willing to put in the effort.

But, you do not want a senior leadership team that focuses on effort. You do not want people who are unable to differentiate 60- to 80-hour work weeks (i.e., "thrashing around") from achieving results.

They will wear themselves (or others) out. They will make avoidable mistakes. You do not (or should not) want to be that leader either.

The best leaders consistently focus on priorities. These leaders understand what their last move was, are clear on where they are now, and know what they need to accomplish next.

A leader who is focused on priorities and results will naturally and consistently do the following:

1. Focus on Personal and Team Clarity

They know what their priority is. They can articulate it clearly and easily without referring to wherever they wrote it down.

2. Forge Alignment

They know the priorities of others, and they create alignment between personal, team, and organizational priorities. Any effort that is spent on unproductive or unaligned activities is scrutinized and, in most cases, set aside for a better time or eliminated.

3. Cultivate Clarity

They help others create clarity about priorities. They ask questions like, "What are we trying to accomplish in this meeting/project/policy?" They ask the Gary Keller question: "What is the one thing, that by so doing, makes everything else easier or unnecessary?"

If you want to build a senior leadership A-Team, you need to have priority-focused leaders. Leaders who know what they are about, what their teams are about, and how to align with each other and leaders who don't tolerate ambiguity.

Anything less is working too hard. For fewer results.

CHAPTER 8

Differences That Make the Difference

Leadership is a potent combination of strategy and character. But, if you must be without one, be without strategy.

— General Norman Schwarzkopf

Leadership Integrity

Credibility is your currency. Do not show up with empty pockets.

A new president or governor's cabinet picks usually consume a lot of media bandwidth. They should. There are questions about how these individuals were selected, their history, their relevant experience and expertise, their character, their ideology, their ability to lead, and their ability to work with others. They go through multiple rounds of vetting and screening.

It is all entirely appropriate. Senior leadership should be chosen with care.

One of the most discouraging experiences for a board, an owner, or an executive is to bring someone into senior leadership who ends up being unreliable or untrustworthy. Sometimes, this feels like a significant disappointment. Sometimes, it comes at great cost to the organization. Sometimes, it can feel like a betrayal.

Minimally, it is inconvenient. In some cases, it is painful. It is often very costly in terms of poor decisions, loss of staff, reputation, or business. If poor leadership is not dealt with in a timely way, the credibility of the rest of the leadership will be called into question.

What Does It Mean to Have Integrity and Credibility?

Integrity is an internal trait. It means there is alignment and consistency between a leader's character, skills, and behaviors. It is a description of what is true about a person.

Credibility is an external trait. It means that a leader is perceived as *doing what they say they will do*. A credible leader needs to not only have integrity but he or she needs to be perceived by others as being reliable, trustworthy, and consistent. It is a description of what others believe to be true about a person.

Your leaders need to have both.

- **Credibility without integrity** is a deception or an illusion. (Depending on who is lying to whom. Sometimes, we do not acknowledge character flaws or the lack of ability in others.)
- **Integrity without credibility** is insipid. Every leader has a reputation. If a leader is the most reliable person in the world, but is not known for it or has a poor reputation, their reliability almost does not matter.
- **Integrity with credibility** is a force to be reckoned with. The leader has the goods and other people know this. No energy or time is wasted on needing to earn trust, prove, or defend oneself. They can focus exclusively on priorities.

Four Questions to Ask to Determine Integrity and Credibility

Do They Do What They Say They Will Do?

Do not make excuses for people. Leadership only happens if there is follow-through. Leaders do not accomplish results through intending or meaning well or making good promises or being distracted. Leaders who have an impact act on their word.

Look for leaders who have demonstrated that they speak with intent and follow through consistently.

What Is Their Track Record?

Do not put someone in senior leadership if they do not have a record of success. Frontline leadership or middle leadership are the places to take a risk or give someone a chance. For senior leadership, you need proven performance with the same (or similar) responsibilities in the same (or similar) context.

Are They Aligned With or Embody Organizational Values?

If *exceptional customer service* is an organizational value, your senior leaders need to *bleed* customer service. It is not enough to give intellectual assent. Customer service has to be something they care so much about they cannot help but show it.

This needs to be true for all your core values. Your senior leaders should be examples of what those values look like in flesh and blood.

Do Their Skills and Aptitudes Match Their Responsibilities?

This is not a character question. It is a capacity question. But, it impacts credibility. It is common to assume that because someone is excellent at X, they might also be good at Y. This too often is not the case. The world is littered with brilliant, but broke attorneys who cannot grow a business, savvy doctors who cannot manage a clinic, motivated and caring board members who cannot read a financial statement.

What to Do with Someone Who Lacks Integrity or Credibility?

If They have Integrity but Lack Credibility

Some people have lost credibility in the past or have behaviors that do not inspire confidence. Assuming they now check out on all four questions above, you are primarily dealing with a perception issue.

The best approach to turn this around is to directly engage those people with whom credibility needs to be built. This takes courage. Which is fine. Leadership is not for cowards.

I typically recommend coaching this person to take the following actions to restore credibility:

- Acknowledge the past issue, directly, to all involved. (Apologize if necessary, without qualifications or minimizers.)
- Identify, specifically, how they intend to act differently.
- Ask for explicit suggestions on what they can start, stop, or do differently.
- Create a specific plan for implementing those behaviors. Communicate that plan to those they lead.
- Have them check in regularly (at least monthly) to see if others feel like they are following through.

I often provide coaching to leaders who want to do well but struggle with a reputation for being too harsh, or inconsistent, self-serving, or some other trait that hampers their ability to work with others. I've found that along with working with the leader grow, we need to work on how they are perceived by others. For this, I use a process called stakeholder-centered coaching, originally developed by Marshall Goldsmith.

It takes a lifetime to build a good reputation. It only takes a moment to lose it. Do not expect restoring one to be easy or a short-term project. But, it can be done. I've typically found that it takes at least a year of consistent work and changed behavior for people to begin to see a leader in a different light.

If any part of this is particularly challenging, I would recommend hiring a coach familiar with stakeholder centered coaching.

If There Is an Integrity Issue

Differentiate if the problem is alignment or interest, capacity, or character.

If it is *alignment or interest*, objectively explore if there is another role or place that might better fit this person. If there is not, you are not doing anyone any favors by keeping or placing them in a position that is not suited for them.

If it is *capacity*, determine if they can quickly be brought up to speed. If they cannot, the position is not a good fit, they will not be able to excel, and it is not fair to set them up for that or make them a burden to others who need them to perform.

If there is a pattern of character or ethical issues, do not even consider them for placement. Let them go if they are already placed. Unethical people are toxic, rarely are willing to change, and should not be in your organization.

Quickly and decisively address the problem.

The longer you tolerate a leader who lacks integrity and credibility, the more you place your credibility at risk.

I often find that leaders ask me about team issues. As I explore what they want to accomplish, they often end up talking about character or performance issues of one of their staff. It is common that these issues have been going on for a while. In some cases, many years.

That is a leadership issue. Not a staff issue. You need to do your job. Do not tolerate a lack of integrity or credibility or yours will come into question— for the right reasons.

Remarkable Leaders Forge Clarity

One of my biggest frustrations as a leader is that the people I lead do not read my mind.

I am pretty sure that if they were conscientious and motivated, they would put effort into figuring out what I want. Even if I have not thought it through yet.

In fact, ideally, people should be able to anticipate anything I want before I get around to wanting it.

Ok, so maybe I'm being a little tongue in cheek. But just a little.

My personal preference, as a leader, is to give people wide berth and manage loosely.

The resulting challenge I have often created is not communicate expectations clearly enough. Often because I haven't defined them for myself. As a result, those that I lead may do things differently than expected, or with a different sense of priority or timing.

As I've grown in my own leadership, this has been one of the primary areas that I've needed to focus on. When I do well in this area, it cleans up all kinds of issues down stream. However, when I don't do this work, problems can be expected to emerge.

The Biggest Leadership Error

The most common leadership error happens when leaders do not create clarity. Ambiguity automatically generates friction, diffusion of energy, or conflict in the system. Or any combination of the three.

You can count on it.

Lack of clarity is so rampant that I can routinely and quickly add 10 percent to 20 percent to nearly any company's bottom line just by helping them get clear in a few basic areas, typically including defining values, the strategic focus, roles and responsibilities, and metrics. There is that much slack in the average company's rope. It really is common sense work, but it often isn't done.

Four Practices of Leaders Who Become Great

We found that for leaders to make something great, their ambition has to be for the greatness of the work and the company, rather than for themselves.

(Great) leaders are a study in duality: modest and willful, humble and fearless.

— Jim Collins

Case Study #1: New CEO

Leader: "I struggle with delegating well."
Myself: "What is it about delegating that you find difficult?"
Leader: "It feels wrong. I don't want to be pushy or manipulative."

Case Study #2: New Director, Large Nonprofit

Myself: "Why don't you communicate your organization's successes and awards for excellence?"
Director: "It comes across as arrogant or boastful."
Myself: "But your organization struggles with a poor reputation (from issues that stopped decades ago). If people have a choice, they go elsewhere and avoid your services."

Director: "We know. It's awful."

As I mentioned earlier, most people struggle with knowing how to relate to humility. Perhaps, it is a cultural issue. Maybe, it is a weakness of the English language.

But few leaders know how to lead well and be humble at the same time.

The Science of Humility and Success

Jim Collins is a researcher and author of bestselling books such as *Good to Great, How the Mighty Fall,* and *Great by Choice.* He became widely popular, in part, because of his counterintuitive research discoveries around success and humility.

Whereas most business or management books are about getting organizations to the top of the bell curve, Jim Collins is interested in greatness. The outstanding outliers on the far-right side of the bell curve.

He found that great companies (those with the highest and consistently sustained success) were all led by the same kind of leader—leaders who were personally humble or modest and fiercely ambitious and motivated about the companies they led.

My Observations of Humility and Arrogance

In my years of consulting experience, I have noticed something about the leaders I have met.

Nearly all of them are intelligent, creative, motivated, and hard-working people. That is the norm.

Not all are leading teams, organizations, or efforts that could be called great.

Some time ago, I decided that I only wanted to work with clients I enjoyed being around and respected.

I also wanted to only work with clients who genuinely valued and deeply cared about their employees and their customers.

The first year where I only took clients who fit that description was a great year. It was my most profitable and most enjoyable year up to that point.

I also began to notice something: as a general rule, these clients are high performers in their industries. They stand out among their peers.

At that time, the economy was down, but most were planning for growth. They also typically experienced high employee engagement and retention.

If they were not great yet, greatness was clearly an option for them.

Upon reflection, these companies have leaders who demonstrate the characteristics of the "modest and willful, humble and fearless" leader that Jim Collins observed.

Not that my clients are perfect or get it right flawlessly. But, they have the desire. They push themselves to the right of the curve.

How to Discern Humble Ambition from Hubris

Whether you are reflecting on this for yourself or considering bringing someone into a more senior position of leadership, watch for these four practices of humbly ambitious leaders.

1.   They Genuinely Enjoy Developing and Promoting the Success of Others

They enjoy success and it doesn't have to be theirs. This might be excited about other people within the organization. It might be other people or organizations in their community. But, they get a natural kick out of someone else doing well and winning. Especially if they were able to be a part of making that happen.

2.   They Confidently and Consistently Communicate the Value or Success of Their Organization without Needing to Compare

There is nothing wrong with communicating that you can receive great service or high-quality product from your company. It is appropriate to communicate and reinforce the value that you offer.

It only becomes hubris once you shift to being *comparative*. "I'm better than that person." "Their services are inferior to ours." "Our department is better run."

3. They are Approachable, Open to Feedback, and Ask for It

Approachable does not mean setting up an open-door policy. Most leaders who tell me they have an open-door policy will also tell me that few people walk through the door.

If you have to tell someone you can be approached, you probably are not approachable.

Most people feel your approachableness. Or the lack thereof.

Humbly ambitious leaders are experienced at being approachable and willing to listen without deflection, excuses, or minimization to feedback (both negative and positive).

The best will take it the next step further and ask, "How can I improve on that next time?" or "What was it that made the experience positive for you?"

Then, they know how to serve even better.

They do not see it only as being criticized or praised. Not that none of that matters. But, these leaders make it about improving their ability to serve.

4. They are Transparent and Authentic About Their Growth Journey

The best leaders I know want growth and pursue growth even though they sometimes fail along the way.

They recognize it is a journey—not just win or fail. They do not see themselves or others as *all good* or *all bad*. They recognize that they are, like everyone else, often a confusing mix.

However, they desire and pursue growth. They develop acceptance and comfort in this and use their own story as encouragement and tool for others.

When selecting senior leadership, choose leaders who demonstrate the four behaviors above. They will naturally grow, inspire others, and pursue the success of the organization.

If you recognize that you would like to grow in one of these areas, develop a plan for growth and follow through. Being humbly ambitious is the differentiator of great leaders from everyone else.

CHAPTER 9

How to Build Your Dream Team

*Hire people who are better than you, then let them get on with it...
Look for people who will aim for the remarkable, who will not settle
for the routine.*

—David Ogilvy

How To Tell If Someone
Is Ready for Senior Leadership

The voice on the phone: "We'd like you to work with Bill. He's one of our supervisors. He has problems working well with other people."

"What makes his ability to work with others important to you and your company?," I ask.

The voice on the phone: "We're grooming him to become the general manager."

"He's not the right guy," I observed.

Leadership Is a Relationship

A leader's relational skills directly correlate with their leadership skills. Highly effective leaders *can* and *do* interact with others effectively. Particularly in times of conflict. Conflict becomes an incredible litmus test of leadership potential.

This is consistently true. How someone relates to conflict is a powerful indicator of their readiness for senior leadership. When selecting or promoting a leader for a senior position, *do not* choose someone who needs remedial work in their social skills. There will not be an end to your regret.

Defining Conflict

People are often confused about what a conflict is. A conflict can be defined as, "any time there is a perceived disagreement over something important to two or more people."

That part is not confusing.

What confuses most people is the false idea that conflict is a failure and something that should always (A) be avoided or (B) be won.

Less effective leaders pick A or B or swing back and forth.

Highly effective leadership recognizes that conflict is an opportunity for growth, for trust to be earned, or to understand others at a deeper level.

Machiavelli Was Wrong

Niccolò Machiavelli was, among other things, an Italian Renaissance political philosopher, politician, and author. He is famous for his book, *The Prince*. In it, he espouses a hyper-pragmatic theory of leadership.

Power is the ability to assert, force, or enforce your will. The Machiavellian approach to life is about the manipulation of power. Gaining and maintaining power. It does not require much of a relationship.

He felt that the real world of politics and leadership was not influenced by ideals, morality, or ethics. So, he advised against being encumbered by them.

Because it is so easy to gain power or position without caring about how you relate to people, many people assume that social competence is optional.

In the short term, this may appear to be an accurate observation. But, it does not play out in the long term. While there is nothing new about someone being able to bully or manipulate their way to the top, that same individual will *always* underperform. What they are able to do well will be countered by all of the drama or distrust they generate because of their poor relational skills.

It takes exponentially more energy and effort for a Machiavellian leader to be effective and to maintain it. They end up wasting an enormous amount of time and resources on political game playing, defending positions, avoiding issues, and fixing mistakes.

Remember, leadership is the ability to intentionally and predictably influence the decisions and actions of others. The most effective leaders rarely choose to utilize power or coercion. They focus on persuasion and influence through relationships and appealing to shared values and vision.

The most effective leaders build healthy relationships based on trust and mutual respect. Then, they can focus their efforts on actually leading. Not on trying to gain or maintain power.

Not convinced? Watch the efforts of many politicians. Particularly those most removed, by distance, from their constituent relationships. There is a strong tendency to focus on this Machiavellian approach. As a result, few accomplish much other than survival in their position. For those who do accomplish more, in terms of legislation or policy change, their accomplishments rarely last because they did not take the time to gain buy-in. Instead, they found a way to force a decision. Which works until someone with more power is able to reverse, defund, or block their decision.

Why is there a tendency toward the Machiavellian approach? Because providing actual leadership is harder to do than achieving a position of leadership. And the U.S. political system primarily rewards those who are able to achieve the position of leadership—not those who are able to provide it. Incidentally, this was intentional. The Founding Fathers understood that if a nation were to choose any kind of revolving leadership model, there would be competition for those positions. They accepted that many of these individuals would be driven by base motivations. The system was built around the assumption that these leaders were primarily looking to further their own interests, not the interests of others, and was designed to force people to find some level of cooperation: Two bodies in Congress, three branches of government. All have to agree for anything to be sustained.

This is often just as true within most organizations. In many cases, the path into leadership is not strongly associated with the ability to lead.

It doesn't mean that everyone utilizes a Machiavellian approach to leadership. But it does mean that if people are promoted or hired into leadership, without having the skills or abilities to lead, they will often use what they have: Which is position or power.

If you are merely selecting for leaders who can hold positions or maintain power, Machiavelli should be on your nightstand. However, if you hope they will genuinely lead and make a difference, you should look elsewhere.

Being Nice Is Also Wrong

If Machiavelli got it wrong, becoming the *nice* leader must be the appropriate approach—right? Wrong.

We all (or most of us) want to be liked and accepted. But leaders who need to be liked, who need to be seen as being nice, who need to please can, also, not just be incredibly ineffective but also damaging.

Being nice is not what you need to look for. Effective leaders will confidently introduce change, confront issues, make hard decisions, or challenge processes. In other words, *conflict is what leaders do.*

I will say that again. Just to be clear: Conflict is what leaders do. This does not always seem nice.

If someone is not good with conflict, they will underdeliver as a leader. A leader who avoids dealing with issues or problem behaviors will never be able to build a healthy, vibrant team. A leader who avoids hard decisions or refuses to challenge "the way things are done" is not leading. They flat out are not leading. Being liked, or nice, is not leadership. Especially, if being nice is about avoiding ruffling feathers.

So, then what?

What to Look for When Choosing Someone for Leadership

Look at these four areas to determine if someone is ready to lead at a higher level. (I go into much greater depth on all of these dynamics in my book *Conflict and Leadership.*)

- **Personal Strength:** Is this person clear on their priorities? Do they have a healthy self-image? Are they motivated by vision (rather than fear?) Are they resilient? Can they relate to and bounce back from disappointment or failure well? Do they seem grateful? Do they strive for personal best vs needing to be better than others?

- **Relationally Competent:** Do they treat others authentically and respectfully? Do they deal with issues in a timely way? Are they able to productively engage in difficult or conflicted conversations? Do they have a track record of pursuing genuine resolution when relationships go sideways? Do they actively build good relationships? Are they free from an unhealthy need for the approval or compliance of others? Are they respected by others (as opposed to being liked or feared)?

- **System and Structure Insight:** Do they ensure that there is an alignment between strategic priorities and how they (and others) structure their calendar or spend their time. Do they ensure that hiring or training processes are in line with strategic goals? Do they clarify roles and responsibilities so that they are relevant to the actual work? Do they structure internal communications so that everyone has easy and timely access to the information they need? Do they create mechanisms or organizational habits to ensure accountability?

- **Culture:** What values are reflected in their decisions or behaviors? Do they reflect organizational values? Is there deep mutual respect and bold honesty among the people they lead? Do they refuse to participate in or tolerate backroom politics? Do they model care and regard for others even in the middle of disagreemetns or challenges? How aware of or intentional are they in shaping the culture around them?

Conflict is a powerful litmus test for leadership. It accentuates strengths and weaknesses. When growing your leaders, look for people who enter into and relate to conflict well. It will save you time and grief while improving the performance of your people.

Twelve Key Traits to Look for When Building a Dream Leadership Team

There is a costly, common mistake that many (perhaps most) organizations make.

Small nonprofits to government agencies to multibillion-dollar businesses. It does not matter.

They build weak senior leadership teams.

The same organizations that are crystal clear about how to hire frontline staff will botch their selection or development of top-level leaders. Of course, this is not intentional. But, when it comes to results, good intentions are not enough.

Why?

Poor leadership selection can happen for a multitude of reasons. Often, it is due to not taking the time to create clarity about what is needed in that role. A very common reason is that the organization grew beneath a certain set of leaders—who did not necessarily grow with the organization. It could also be due to feeling like someone has earned the position due to loyalty or longevity (both are poor reasons to select a leader.)

Whatever the reasons may be, the costs of a poor decision are high.

Costs of Poor Leadership Selection

And by high, I mean dramatically so. The wrong leadership decision can be expected to result in:

- Increased employee turnover
- Decreased employee morale
- Customer dissatisfaction and attrition
- Decrease in employee productivity
- Turf battles and silos

It is so predictable; you can plan on it. Poor leaders = poor results.

All of this translates into measurable costs financially. It limits your ability to accomplish your strategic goals or your focus. At a minimum, time, energy, resources, knowledge, and relationships are all directed away from the purposes of the organization toward the issues generated by poor leadership.

As a result, you might take longer to get where you need to go. Or, you might be hamstrung and not able to get there at all.

So, let us avoid that. You can do this by screening for the 12 specific leadership traits when you build your leadership team.

Twelve Traits for Your Dream Team

These 12 traits are universally applicable, across industry, size, or age of organization. Look for these traits in the experience, reputation, and success of the people you are considering. *Past experience is the best indicator of future performance.* Senior leadership is not the place for someone to begin exploring their leadership capacity. They should be chosen on demonstrated capacity. Look for this:

1. **Active Leaders or Initiators:** Good leaders actually lead. They do not sit back, make suggestions, or focus on mentoring. All good things. But, active leaders bring about direction, clarity, and focus. They ensure that issues are addressed, projects are started and progress is tracked. They end things that need ending.

2. **Manage Outcomes:** They are focused on what is supposed to be accomplished. They do not confuse activity for results. They differentiate 80-hour work weeks from eight productive hours. They know what outcomes their teams and staff are supposed to accomplish and manage to those ends.

3. **Integrity and Credibility:** The best leaders know that *credibility* is a leader's currency. If a leader's instincts, intent, capacity, and judgment are trusted, there is little they cannot get their team to do. If any of the above is doubted, the leader is his or her own worst enemy. A good leader actively builds and generates credibility. *Never* select a deceptive person or someone who does not follow through.

4. **Technically Interested and Literate:** The best leaders know how to talk to their teams in language the teams use. They do not need to be experts in the technical details. But, in terms of communication and

understanding context, leaders should learn to talk to and understand their team.

5. **Easily Manage Priorities:** Time management is priority management. A leader who manages time well will also be clear about their priorities *and* can make their priorities clear to others. A leader who does not manage their own time well will not be clear about their priorities or the priorities of anyone else.

6. **Effectively Addresses Conflict and Weirdness:** Good leaders deal with issues in a way that both preserves the dignity of others and is also decisive. They do not sweep things under the rug; they do not hope it will go away or fix itself. If there is an elephant in the room, it gets dealt with until it is resolved.

7. **Creates Clarity:** Good leaders always ask clarifying questions. Their expectations are clear. Their vision feels both lofty and tangible. You know what they are talking about. They are willing to explain themselves until others understand. They have a low tolerance for ambiguity. They know that in the absence of clarity, there is confusion or conflict. If clarity does not exist, they create it.

8. **Ambitious Humility:** The most effective leaders are those who combine a high level of ambition for their teams or organizations with personal humility. These leaders are driven, motivated, and willing to make hard decisions, but also care about others, are teachable, and able to be corrected. They do not see their position as being *over* others but instead see themselves as facilitating the success of others.

9. **Forges Unity:** The best leaders will always find a way to accomplish mutual beneficiality. They resist factions or silos. They do not engage in turf politics. They understand (or insist on identifying) the core focus, purpose, or strategy of the organization and align their efforts toward that. They work to bring others into alignment as well.

10. **See Growth and Opportunity:** This has to do with perspective and mindset.

    Growth: Most people think in terms of maintaining a status quo. You need people who think of growth and improvement.

    Opportunity: You need senior leaders who can find opportunity in tough situations and do not miss the right opportunity in good situations. Not many people can see opportunities.

11. **Resilience:** Resilient leaders are not dumbstruck, shattered, or shut down with challenges, adversity, or failure. They know how to summon resources, reflect on what was learned, recover their footing, and move on ahead—stronger for the experience.

12. **Teachable:** The very best leaders are always learning and are open to correction. As a result, they have probably developed a high level of competence and confidence in a number of areas. However, they still remain open to learning and being taught more. They know how to manage and consider critical feedback. They do not let pride prevent them from listening to others.

Your senior leadership selection is a *key hire* process. Take the time to make sure you have chosen the best.

Their Value Should Be Noticeable

When your new senior leader gets his or her shoulder under the organizational burden, everyone should feel the benefit of their effort. They should meaningfully contribute to lifting the organization.

The right new leader brings ideas, energy, solutions, and connections. They make things happen. They make your job easier. They help others succeed.

If they do not do these things quickly, they are the wrong person for that position.

How to Tell if a Leader Will Produce Growth

I recently heard from an executive who was struggling in a tight situation. Her staff was overworked. She had tapped out her revenue opportunities. She felt trapped in a catch-22 of, "I need resources so that I can grow. I need growth so that I have resources."

She keeps coming to mind. When she does, I feel sad. She works in the fastest and most robust growth industry in the country. There should be nothing but potential in front of her. Despite this, she only sees the obstacles.

I cannot get her to return my calls. That is why, I feel sad. I know her company well. I know there are real challenges that she faces. But, she is only held back by her mindset. Growth is possible, she wants it, but she is blocked by how she sees or interprets her world. And, that is the truth.

She'll stay stuck until she is willing to challenge her mindset. If she is stuck, so is the entire company. Everyone else who has career hopes and dreams. Every client who could and should receive more, better, or new services. Every stakeholder who has a vested interest in the company's success.

They cannot go beyond her mindset.

This is why it is an absolute necessity for senior leaders to be people who possess a mindset of growth and the ability to see opportunities.

To lead means to go first. Sometimes, this means to go first with your imagination or vision. I cannot lead anyone to somewhere I cannot imagine. If I cannot see or imagine or discern or identify opportunities, I will never lead to them.

Most people think in terms of the status quo. They might want to maintain it because it is familiar. They may just not be able to see anything beyond *what is*. That is the norm.

But, those people don't lead. Although they can fill the space of a leadership positions.

Find someone who has demonstrated an ability to see opportunity and produce growth.

The Precious, Precious Mindsets of Growth and Opportunity: Five Indicators

Here is what to look for.

1. They Find Opportunities in Tough Situations

When times are tough, there is a tendency for people to focus on pain points. Many people shift to fatalism: "I hope things get better." "We can't do anything about the economy." "The government should do something." Others shift to victim-stance: "I inherited a mess." "My team just doesn't step up." Some get stuck in second-guessing: "I don't want to make a mistake."

The best leaders recognize challenges, but they own the situation and look for ways to make things better. They turn their teams around. They create opportunities if none present themselves. They pursue imperfect progress. They are resilient.

2. They Act on the Right Opportunity in Good Situations

When times are good, it is easy to coast. It is easy to say, "What got us here will probably get us anywhere else." It is easy to feel that good opportunities will wait. They misjudge the thin line between feeling comfortable and being complacent.

The best leaders actively look to move from strength to strength. They do not look for opportunities to coast. They look for opportunities to leverage. They understand that organizations are organisms. They require movement and growth to be healthy.

3. They Prepare and Position Themselves for Opportunity

Many wait for opportunities to crawl up and go to sleep in their lap before they get ready for them. Teams, finances, and structures are all designed and set up to handle, *now.* (Or even worse—*yesterday.*) There is no built-in capacity or readiness for growth when the opportunity presents itself.

More leaders are willing to prepare themselves for disaster (which they can more readily imagine) than for growth.

The best leaders are constantly readying themselves and their teams for opportunities. They create margin so that they can act. They work with their teams to think forward. They train and grow to handle more. They build systems and foundations that can support more.

4. They Are Innovative

Status quo leaders can only offer used ideas. When situations change, they will keep trying to do the same thing. Blockbuster ignored streaming video. Netflix didn't. Sears ignored the Internet. Amazon didn't.

The best leaders innovate. Innovation is rarely a thought completely unlike any other thought ever. More often, innovative leaders combine two *used* ideas and make something new (gourmet chocolate bars with bacon). They discover new applications or audiences for an old idea (Lego movies that target adults). Inventing is good, but innovating is faster and easier.

5. They are Ready to Act

My most successful clients relentlessly execute. They act. They don't dither. Too many leaders want results but won't act. They are most often afraid of making a mistake, failing, or conflict. This is a common reason smart people do not follow through on great (or even just halfway decent) ideas.

I worked with a client for six years. When I started they were a single small team. By my last engagement, they had grown into multiple states and were national leaders in their industry. They work in an industry that has a very well understood path to success. They had access to the same training, coaching, and support as everyone else. But very few attain real success in this industry. Their difference? They actually did it. They act.

The best leaders are resilient. Resilience allows action. They realize that most of us are not brain surgeons, and most of our work can tolerate some error. They realize it is better to fix and improve something that has started than to miss your opportunity by never starting.

If you are recruiting or hiring someone for senior leadership, look for mindsets of growth and opportunity.

It is healthy to have a team that can question and challenge new ideas as part of a decision vetting process. It is unhealthy (to the point of being fatal) to have a team that only sees obstacles and prefers to shoot down anything that looks new or feels unfamiliar.

How to Know if a Leader Is Teachable

I know a man who is the most gifted handyman I have ever met. He can repair, remodel, or rebuild anything. He is a craftsman in the truest sense of the word and takes pride in his workmanship.

One day, he told me that he often does not know how to do the jobs that he is hired to do. But, he knows what he can figure out and if he can figure them out in time. His greatest skill is his ability to quickly learn and then solve problems.

Leaders should be the same way. There is no way for a leader to be effective by only working with challenges and issues they already understand. Leaders, almost by definition, have to be able to forge a path through unknown territory. They have to be able to figure things out.

Therefore, they have to be learners. They have to be teachable.

The Value of a Learning Leader

Technology moves fast. So does the economy. What you learned 10 or 20 years ago may no longer be the most relevant or useful information, skills, or techniques. For that matter, what you learned last year might already be aged.

Because of this dynamism, it is no longer possible (if it ever was) to master your craft and never have to learn again. Instead, a crucial leadership skill and attitude to cultivate in ourselves and look for in our key hires is the ability and passion to *learn*.

A leader who is constantly pushing, constantly trying to grow in his or her abilities and understanding, is someone who you can count on to adapt and adjust to change, growth, or challenges.

We Depend on Learning Leaders

It is rare to meet someone who will tell you, "I'm not interested in learning or bettering myself." Instead, most people will present themselves as if they are learners. However, this is not always true.

I used to serve on the licensing board for psychologists in my state. To maintain licensure, all psychologists are required to complete a certain amount of continuing education every two years. This is normal in many professions. Fortunately, for most psychologists, this was not an issue. Many are curious people who genuinely want to grow and improve in their ability to serve their clients.

But, there were always some who were not. Some who put more effort and time into creating excuses rather than attend a couple workshops a year. It was only with the threat of losing their license that they would finally crack open a book or attend a class.

Their lack of professional initiative and interest was always surprising to me. These are highly educated people. They spent an enormous part of their lives in school. But, they did not seem to love to learn or grow. They were always looking for the minimum level of requirements or effort.

Unfortunately, there was no way to add the tag, *lazy and indifferent*, to a psychologist's license. But, I bet their clients or employers would like to know.

The Six Key Behaviors of Learning Leaders

So, how do we know if someone is a *learning leader*? What do we look for to determine whether someone is adaptable, curious, and motivated?

What are the key indicators of someone who will not just keep up with change, but lead it?

Here are the five behaviors that I believe you should look for.

1. *Are they curious?* Do they ask questions? Do they actively try to understand things? When they do not understand something, do they stop and ask for clarification? When they are introduced to a new idea, tool, or approach, do they seem genuinely interested? Do they explore it with you? Do they ask for more information so they can follow up later?

When they discover the success of others, what do they talk about? Do they explore what that person or team did to build success? Do they tell others about how that person or organization succeeded?

Exploring the success of others demonstrates a desire and ability to learn. Broadcasting the success of others indicates the assumption that others want to learn and grow as well (which is insight into their attitude).

Both indicate a level of humility.

2. *How well do they pay attention?* What do they do with their phone when they meet with you? Do they allow themselves to be interrupted? How interested do they appear to be? What is the quality of their follow-up questions?

What do they pay attention to? How well (and for how long) can any one thing hold their attention? Do they seem to be aware of their environment? What about trends in relevant parts of the economy, market, or community?

While it is fine to be entertained, does it appear they spend more time paying attention to their favorite sports team or TV show than their team or organizational health?

Learners are attentive. They know their attention has limited bandwidth. Look for behaviors that show they protect how that bandwidth is used.

3. *Are they learning something right now?* Learners cannot help but learn new things. And, they are learning right now. Not just when they are required to.

Do they seem to be learning in their current position? Do they assess and evaluate and reflect on lessons learned? Are they looking for and pursuing opportunities to grow?

What they are learning does not have to exclusively be in their area of expertise. Is someone learning about gardening? A new parenting approach? Are they dabbling in carpentry? Are they taking a cooking class?

Specifically, look for someone who has made learning and growing a normal part of their life.

4. *Do they talk about what they are learning?* I know a mediator who is, unsurprisingly, also an attorney. He is also an engineer and has recently completed his doctorate in psychology.

He was in his seventies when he started his doctoral work. While going through his studies, he was so enthusiastic about what he was learning. It just leaked out of him. He did not need the degrees or titles. His career had been set multiple times over. He just loved to learn new things.

When he shared what he was learning, it was not from an attitude of superiority. It was from a place of excitement and the belief that others might be as excited as he was.

Look for people who cannot help but talk about something new they are learning. Especially when it just bubbles up out of their enthusiasm for the topic. They might not frame it as, "I'm learning this." But, they might talk about a new hobby, or a challenge they overcame, or a book they recently read.

5. *Are they being taught?* Some people are learners, but they are not open to being taught.

I worked with someone who was a learner, but he insisted on learning *his way*. As a result, the lessons he learned were often wrong or not that useful. He was resistant to having others adjust or correct his understanding or approaches.

As a result of being overly impressed with his exceptionalism, he spent far more time than necessary in the *school of hard knocks*.

Look for leaders who have coaches, instructors, or teachers. It is an indication that they are willing to receive instruction and guidance. It is another indication of humility. It also means that they are willing to receive help and not just learn on their terms.

Look for leaders who can be taught by the people they lead. Some leaders have a naïve belief that they should never show weakness.

Their staff has probably already figured out what they are not good at. Look for someone who does not hide it (they are not fooling anyone), but instead asks for help.

6. *Do they spend time with people "ahead" of them?* A runner will run faster if she is not the fastest person in the race.

A leader who wants or needs to be the smartest person in the room is someone who has put a limit on their growth or abilities. The leader who does that limits the success or growth of their teams or organizations.

Look for leaders who regularly and intentionally surround themselves with people are ahead of them—in skills, knowledge, success, and so on.

The Best Leaders Are Learners

There is no way you can anticipate all of the changes, challenges, or opportunities you will face. Make sure you have built a team of people who can face them with you. The very best of these will be people who make learning part of their lifestyle.

Five Habits of Resilient Leaders

In college, I worked with people who experienced developmental disabilities. Part of my job was called *community inclusion*. Many of our clients had a difficult time getting involved in the community and faced social stigmas when they did so. So, we helped them overcome this.

One day, I was assigned to work with a man I will call Keith. My assignment was to meet with him a couple times a week to help him get out into the community, stay on top of bills, shopping, and so on.

Keith was born with a developmental disability. He also has a physical disability from being run over by a car. He lives with his wife, who also has a developmental disability.

Keith is one of those *cop geeks*. He loves all things cop. He listens to the police radio, wears tactical pants, and uses cop words. I have known a lot of people like that. Most go nowhere beyond vicariously connecting with law enforcement.

As it turned out, Keith had an actual relationship with every police officer we came across. Not only that, he was an active member of the local community patrol and the civil air patrol.

Before I got to know him well, I made the mistake of assuming he was humored by many of these groups. Far from it. Whenever we bumped into someone he knew around town (which was a regular occurrence), their faces lit up, and they wanted to talk. He was very much a part of each of these groups.

I wasn't. I was essentially ignored whenever we met someone he knew. I was clearly not *in*. I was not a relevant part of how they experienced Keith. If anything, I needed Keith to help me get included.

As Keith and I built a friendship, he told me he was grateful for his disabilities. I was surprised to hear this. He told me that because of his disabilities, he received many great resources and services and had opportunities that were not as readily available for others.

Most people would view him as disadvantaged. Keith did not see it that way. Keith was rich in relationships. He was also active in serving and giving. In fact, when it comes to living life fully, there are many people without disabilities, living far more anemic lives than Keith.

Keith is resilient. As a result, he lives more, and he offers more.

Your Leaders Need to Demonstrate Resilience

Resilience is the ability to bounce back or recover from difficulties. It is toughness. It is grit.

I am often surprised by what stops people. Particularly those in leadership positions. So many just stop when they encounter an obstacle, a setback, an unknown situation, a fear.

These people remain victims of their circumstances.

That is not leadership.

All leaders, but senior leaders particularly, need to be resilient. They need mental toughness. They need grit. They need to be able to be knocked back, knocked down, and then get back up better for it.

This speaks to their character, the core stuff they are made of. Without it, they cannot be counted on to overcome obstacles or challenges. They cannot be counted on to lead when leadership is most needed.

Do not bring someone into senior leadership who is not resilient. Someone who lets their decisions be driven by fear instead of vision. Who stalls or makes excuses instead of facing fears and uncertainties. Someone who quits when the going gets hard.

Their resume might be great. They might have a lot of industry knowledge. They could have impressive accomplishments. They could be very nice and have lots of great relationships.

But when things are difficult, you need someone you can rely on.

The Five Practices of Resilient Leaders

1. Resilient Leaders Rewrite Their Story

The story I was given about Keith was that he was disabled, alone, and needed my help.

The story that Keith gave himself was that he was engaged, involved, contributing, and connected and willing to let me tag along. It was a convenience for him that I had a car to drive him around in. But, he would have been just fine with the bus or riding his bicycle.

Resilient people take the same set of facts but focus on opportunities. Instead of getting stuck on frustrations, they see what can be appreciated. Instead of fixating on what they cannot do, they find advantages.

Resilient leaders control their story.

Resilient leaders actively shape the narrative for themselves and those they lead. The shape it toward growth, learning, overcoming, and abundance.

2. Resilient Leaders Face Fears

When something goes bump in the dark, resilient leaders do not hide under the covers sipping air through a monster snorkel. Unfortunately, many organizations and leadership teams develop fantastic methods of doing just that.

Resilient leaders may experience the normal feelings that others do: For example, if experiencing something new and unknown. They may feel fear or uncertainty.

But they don't get stuck on those feelings. They flip the lights on and investigate the closets and under the bed. They face their fears.

They ask the next question instead of pulling back. They challenge assumptions. They become concerned when strategy is developed based on risk aversion and *what ifs* as opposed to vision or values.

Fear usually disappears with a little light.

3. Resilient Leaders Take Care of Themselves

I used to have a roommate. I will call him James. Whenever he made a mistake, he would slap himself on the forehead and say, "Stupid! Stupid! Why did I do that?" or, "Typical James!"

I am sure many of us have had negative self-talk. There is no instance of it being helpful. Ownership of a problem or mistake is good. But, wallowing in that ownership is not. Ownership should only be an early step to growth and avoiding similar problems in the future.

Resilient leaders:

Have Self-Awareness:

They recognize how they are feeling and responding to issues.

Cultivate Perspective and Proportionality:

They see things for what they are and respond accordingly. The do not make mountains out of molehills. They do not avoid, hide, excuse, or minimize.

Take Care of Themselves:

They do not redline. They do not burn themselves out. They are not trying to be martyrs. They learn to rest, recharge, regain focus, and perspective. They do not need to be told to do these things.

4. Resilient Leaders Learn:

When difficulties happen, particularly when they repeat themselves, resilient leaders learn from the experience.

They learn how to grow personally. They learn how to build, prepare, or repair trust and credibility in relationships. They learn what does and does not work in terms of team or organizational structures, practices, or policies. They reflect on how organizational culture helps or hinders and make changes accordingly.

5. Resilient Leaders Let Go

They forgive. They do not hold onto grudges. They do not pursue revenge. They do not find someone to blame.

Resilient leaders do not need the energy that anger, resentment, or bitterness creates for some people. They are fueled by the vision of what they are trying to build.

They are not living reactively.

Forgiveness is not easy. But, to not be able to let go means giving over control of some level of your emotions or choices to a past event or someone who wronged you. It gives control of your future to something from the past.

Resilient people are aware of their past. They take care of themselves. They set healthy boundaries if needed. They learn.

They move on.

When building your team, look for people with track records of resilience. Anyone can be a good sailor in calm weather. You need people who keep their head in a storm.

PART IV

First Things

CHAPTER 10

Starting Out Right

Leaders must always operate with the understanding that they are part of something greater than themselves and their own personal interest.

—Jocko Willink

The First Four Priorities for a New Executive

In high school, I played basketball. Our varsity team had won state championship for two years, back to back. Then, the head coach moved away. A new coach was hired. From the way he related to us, it felt like he saw himself as Gene Hackman's character in *Hoosiers*. He was going to be the tough coach that whips his group of losers into shape.

Except we were already champions.

Within a few short months, he whipped us into a place of such low morale that the entire starting five threatened to quit. I did quit. We did not even place at Regions. He killed the team. He killed his credibility. For reasons unknown, the school retained him. He was never able to rebuild the team.

How he entered his leadership role set the course for failure or success.

New leaders make various kinds of entrances into their role. Experience, personality, confidence, maturity, and history (or lack thereof) with the team or organization all play a part in this.

Fortunately, the model for an effective entrance is very straightforward. It also benefits from being broadly applicable. In other words, this is the right approach for stepping into a healthy organization or a distressed one. It is the right approach when promoted into the executive role or hired from outside.

It is just the right approach. Following these steps will help you quickly gain credibility and the loyalty of those you lead. It will mitigate the potential disruption that comes with a leadership change. It will help you avoid many of the minefields that some new leaders seem determined to wander through.

The Model for an Effective Executive Entrance

Priority #1: Inventory Strengths

This first step is to take an inventory of what the team or organization does or has done well. Review what has worked in the past and what is working well now. This both gives you useful information and goodwill. There are a number of ways to go about this.

The first I will call the *Green method*. Brian Green is the executive director of what can most easily be described as a "holding company" for a group of non profits primarily focused on health care.

He was a mentor of mine in my first role as an executive in a tiny, struggling non profit. When we had meetings, he would often recite his inventory of successes and strengths in my life. Then he was interested if there was anything new to add to the list.

We don't see each other as often now, perhaps once every one or two years. But when we connect, he does the same thing. We meet at a restaurant or coffee shop, he'll greet me with a hug and then launch into a recitation of my successes—both professional and personal. It is after this that we catch up.

I'm not the kind of person that needs a lot of buttering up. But I'll admit, it always feels good. I know (and he knows) that there are struggles and challenges that I face—like everyone else. But he builds the conversation on strengths.

I don't know if he started doing this on purpose or if it just comes out of him. Either way, it's a brilliant way to begin a conversation. Or in the context of a new CEO—beginning a new relationship. By both researching past successes and elements of personal or organizational pride and salting those findings into your conversations, you will accomplish two goals: *First,* you will reassure people that you respect the same things they respect and value. By doing this, you will reduce the normal anxiety many people feel around change. *Second,* you will gather useful information about what this group of people does well. This allows you to build on existing strengths rather than attempt to start from scratch.

Another way to do this (it is worth using both approaches) is asking a few questions that come from the technique called *appreciative inquiry.* This approach was developed by David Cooperrider, a professor at Case Western Reserve University. People enjoy answering these questions. It also is a simple but powerfully effective way to shift people into a very positive mindset. I often use it, especially when engaging with a group that struggles with confidence or internal conflicts. They are also very effective as part of a coaching process.

I won't introduce the entire process here. But the idea is to use strengths and successes as a starting point for leading change or planning (as opposed to the more typical "pain point" or "what needs to be fixed" approach.)

I walk the leader(s) through a series of questions or topics that move something like this:

- Describe a time that we have been at our best as a team or organization.
- What was it about us (our qualities, habits, behaviors, skills, etc.) that made being at our best possible?
- What do you value most about this organization? This team? This project? Your role?
- What do you think the core values or characteristics of the organization are? What makes you unique and different from others doing similar work?
- If you had three wishes for the organization, what would they be?

This can be done with individuals or with a group. The process is powerful because it is so nonthreatening. But, it digs deep into what is really important for people. It starts at a place of strength and positive remembrances. It allows people to project forward from this place of "We have succeeded" to "We do succeed" to "We will succeed."

Even though it is never directly asked, it also unearths challenges or fears through the question of the *three wishes.* So, if change is needed, even difficult change, you will unearth that. (Some people stress about not talking about what's not working—I always have to reassure them that we'll get off the good stuff eventually and get into the ugly.)

By starting out by building this positive inventory, your eventual conversation about challenges is from a place where people feel optimistic and, importantly, not threatened. By doing so, you have reduced concerns that are common when new leaders start.

I have often advised new CEOs to set up interviews with their staff, ask these questions, and just listen. It's powerful.

Identify Interests: Review Desires and Goals for the Future

If you follow the process described above, you will have already started gathering this information. I have written a lot on the critical importance of identifying interests, in particular when resolving conflicts. Interests are nothing more than very core desires, hopes, or concerns that someone has. They could show up anywhere in the conversation above—but they are generally clearest in the "Three Wishes" question.

If you report to anyone, you will want to know what it is that they want. Sometimes, they know exactly what they want. In my experience, though, many owners or boards have not really thought it through to the level of detail that gives you meaningful direction.

So, you need to ask for it.

Reviewing desires and interests is critically important when engaging the motivation of your workforce. You will get the best out of people when organizational goals are connected to what drives or motivates them personally.

- In fact, I would recommend having a one-on-one conversation with at least each member of your direct reports, but also as many levels down as you can. In this conversation, you should ask people specifically:
- What are one or two things that we do great that we should protect?
- What are one or two areas that we should grow in or change?

There is some skill in asking these questions. Many people will offer a specific idea or position: "I think we should pursue XYZ contract." Or

"I think we should change the ABC policy." It helps to explore this and ask, "What makes that important to you?" or "What do you think the consequences of not doing that will be?"

This helps you understand what it is really important to people, which makes it easier for you to effectively lead them and tie into their motivations.

Identify Quick Wins: Pick Low-Hanging Fruit

I am referring to *really* low-hanging fruit. The wins do not have to be large. If there are annoyances, frustrations, or inconveniences that everyone has been living with that you can easily address—address them. If there is a simple opportunity you can take advantage of—do it. If there is an easy PR win you can achieve (that focuses on the organization, not yourself)—make it happen.

Important Point

While it is natural for you to be in the spotlight, ideally, these wins are not about you gaining more spotlight. Not to say that you should not win a contract, build a key relationship, or solve a problem. But, your personal success is best demonstrated through your team's success.

Sometimes, these quick wins are much simpler than you think. In fact, there may be small wins happening all around you that no one is recognizing. It is not uncommon to find that a particular department or team has quietly been doing fantastic work that has gone unacknowledged. Just highlighting this, and blowing their trumpet for them, will mean much more than you think.

Vision: Create an Organizing, Longer-Term Focus

While it is often fine to come into your position with a vision for the future, it may be a delicate time to announce anything that seems like major changes. That is, unless you know these changes are wanted within the organization.

Usually, you will not know that unless you have done the work aforementioned. And, even if you know that, you will want to make sure that you have built sufficient credibility to be able to accomplish the work that needs to be done.

There is rarely a good reason that you cannot accomplish the steps aforementioned within the first month or two. Definitely within the first quarter. A good goal is to accomplish as much of this before your *honeymoon* ends. Which can be faster than you might hope.

One of the most important and distinguishing skills of a leader is the ability to create a *vision for the future* that inspires others. This does not need to be your 10-year vision of world conquest. In fact, it often makes more sense to have a vision that may only be in the 9- to 18-month range. But, it should be big enough to be meaningful to everyone. It also provides focus for everyone. It gives you a tool to nurture alignment throughout the organization.

Start Smart

Looking back, the new basketball coach missed these opportunities. As a result, the associate coaches stepped back and took a more passive role. The team itself went into revolt. He spent more time trying to rebuild what was not originally broken than building on what was already there.

Any of the steps of this model take a little bit of effort. Sometimes, it may seem it requires vulnerability. It definitely benefits from humility.

In practice, most of this model can be integrated within the course of normal business. In fact, in many cases, you will find that people actually prefer that you take this time.

Start out by charting your course, building a relationship with the crew, and keeping your hand on the helm. You will spend far less time in the doldrums, lost, bailing water, and managing mutinies later on.

Secrets of Success for New CEOs

The global consulting firm, McKinsey, conducted a study[1] of CEOs to identify if there was a connection between early, big decisions and overall

---

[1] Birshan, M., T. Meakin, and K. Strovink. 2018. "How New CEOs can Boost Their Odds of Success." *McKinsey Quarterly*. accessed August 8, 2018.

success (as defined by total return to shareholders). What they found is enlightening.

What Decisions Have the Most Impact?

According to the study, most incoming CEOs tend to make similar strategic choices or moves in their first two years, at roughly the same rates. This is regardless of whether the company was successful or struggling. Their strategic choices, in percentage of frequency, follow:

New CEO strategic moves	Successful companies	Struggling companies
Management reshuffle	66%	72%
Merger or acquisition	59%	54%
Cost-reduction program	42%	49%
New business or product launch	38%	37%
Geographic expansion	26%	32%
Organizational redesign	26%	29%
Business/product closure	19%	18%
Strategic review	14%	31%
Geographic contraction	9%	5%

Although the decisions had similar frequencies, their efficacy changed depending on whether the company was already successful or struggling.

Top Three Decisions That Created Situational Success

1. **Organizational redesign** was the decision that had the greatest impact on already *successful companies*. Despite this, this choice was only made 26 percent of the time. Surprisingly, it had little impact on low performers.

   Explore: If you are are leading an already successful company there may be a temptation to avoid tinkering with what is working. But even the best athletes are always looking for ways to improve their form, their technique or their edge. Success, surprisingly to some, often generates growth or change. Your organization may need to grow or change to sustain success.

2. **Strategic reviews** had the greatest impact on *struggling* companies. However, it was only chosen by 31 percent of CEOs at struggling companies. This appears to be an underutilized decision. The impact of initiating a strategic review was limited for already successful companies, perhaps because they were more likely to already have this process in place.

Explore: I have found that accountability and regularly reviewing progress, at least quarterly, helps many of my struggling clients turn themselves around. Companies commonly struggle because they don't know how they are performing. They aren't sure what their goals are, don't know how to measure them, and don't want to talk about it.

Additionally, if you are successful, and don't currently have this practice, you might consider starting to improve the likelihood of sustaining your success.

3. **Reshuffling management teams** often produced a significant benefit for struggling businesses. However, this choice destroyed value in already successful companies. Caution: This was the most common choice made by incoming CEOs. If taking the helm at an already successful company, do not be so quick to make management changes.

Explore: The impact of leadership and management are real. A poorly performing company is nearly always poorly led or managed at some level. If these leaders or managers won't change, they usually need to be changed if different performance is wanted.

But, if the company is successful, be cautious changing how it is led or who is leading it. If not done well, and for a good reason, it can communicate a disregard for the existing success and the people who created or sustained it—not to mention the loyalty many people feel towards their leaders (but not necessarily to you, yet.) It tends to damage moral, could boost turnover, loss of institutional knowledge, and so on.

An Observation

New CEOs frequently made disruptive and unproductive choices such as reshuffling management in successful companies. What may seem obvious or expedient may not be.

Additionally, according to this study, some of the choices made less frequently (such as strategic reviews in struggling companies) proved to be some of the most valuable.

Decision-Making Principles for New CEOs

The study made several other observations:

- **Think like an outsider:** Whether the company is performing well or poorly, most CEOs will make a significant, strategic change. A big move. Interestingly, the CEOs hired from the outside (which are the minority) tended to make more of these big moves.

  In my experience, inside hires are often hampered by fear of rocking the boat relationally, internal politics, and the same blind spots that created the problems to begin with. Outsiders do not come in with those relationships or baggage. They see things differently and so feel free to act differently.

  This does not mean outside CEOs are better. They will lack institutional knowledge and understanding of the organizational culture. But, it does mean that if you were hired from within, you should seek and be open to outside perspectives.

- **Make decisions aligned with company values, vision, and desired outcomes.** Some new CEOs try to follow a successful manual or pattern. Sometimes, this is attempting to replicate a successful mentor they look up to, or a successful peer in their field.

  It can feel safe or expedient to copy what others are doing, hoping to mimic their success.

  It is helpful to look at what others are doing. That is getting the outside perspective.

  However, it is best to look at the underlying principles of their success as opposed to seeking for a success blueprint to follow. The success of others is often influenced by variables outside of easy observation and control. In other words, trying to do exactly what *they* did will often not work.

Your decisions should be based on what makes the most sense given your starting point, environment, and desired outcomes.

The best answers are usually innovations—learning lessons from others, but adapting those lessons to best fit your context and goals. Be discerning when mimicking tactics and cautious about mimicking strategy. When doing so, focus on principles rather than exact replication.

- **For struggling organizations, think comprehensively.** The most successful turnarounds in struggling organizations came from CEOs who made more than four big changes in a two-year period.

  In other words, they realized "It's a big boat, we'd better turn fast and turn hard before we're far off course."

  Successful companies saw a smaller benefit from change and did not require as many changes. Regardless, successful changes in any context were made strategically and carefully, presumably in response to the strategic review. They were made with a *whole organization* context. While fast and large, they were not reactive.

  Not making a big move, or a number of big moves, is often the worst choice.

They Say Change is Hard. Not Changing Might Be Harder

Not making the big changes is why:

- Blockbuster is not Netflix
- Sears is not Amazon
- RadioShack is not Best Buy

Timely and strategically led big changes allow for continued growth. Do not be shy about doing what needs to be done.

How to Avoid the Most Common Rookie Leadership Errors

There are many paths to executive leadership. However, when beginning a new role, many new leaders use one of the four following approaches.

Each of these falls short and ultimately creates more work for the leader later on.

The Four Unhelpful Approaches for New Leaders

Approach #1: There is a New Sheriff in Town

This phrase is derived from American, or at least Hollywood, lore of the Old West. A town is controlled by the baddies. There is corruption. People do not feel safe. There is lots of mud and shooting and people getting thrown out of taverns.

Then the new sheriff shows up. Cleans up the town, gets rid of the baddies, the taverns encourage polite card games, and the mud dries up.

Sometimes, an organization genuinely does need a turnaround. Sometimes, that turnaround needs to happen quickly with, can I say, aggressiveness. But a *shoot-em-up* approach to making big changes will do more damage than help.

A new leader may recognize that real change is needed. That leader may have a strong, new vision for the future. But our new sheriff does not yet know how to moderate his or her approach to the actual circumstances. Tough decisions may be needed. But if "making tough decisions" is your primary strategy, it'll backfire.

As a result, people leave, resist, or get passive. It is surprising to me how commonly this is a tolerated cost of business. Particularly, high turnover.

In most cases, there is an expectation and acceptance of high turnover as a result of new leadership. This is sloppy and irresponsible. An organization is losing too much in training, institutional knowledge, and relationships. Some turnover is unavoidable, but high turnover following a leadership transition means no one wants to work in the environment they expect you will create. Unless you are getting rid of a lot of awful employees, high turnover is usually a signal of something going wrong.

The result is that it is not uncommon for the new sheriff to get completely derailed from accomplishing their cleanup or vision building. They get stuck in having to rebuild the *town* that they shot up and tore apart.

Solution

Be cautious and humble before labeling opposition, confusion, unsettled loyalties or resistance as a sign of *baddies*. Recognize the past success, existing strengths, values, and culture of individuals and the organization. Even when a turnaround is needed, you will be more effective if you build on strengths.

Approach #2: Everybody's Buddy

Many new leaders want to be friends. Maybe they were promoted up and are now leading people who were peers. Maybe they are new to town or the organization and genuinely are looking for relationships.

I believe emotional intelligence is one of the most important skill sets for a leader. Research supports this. However, it is important to have a mature understanding of how this is expressed as a leader. Being a buddy does not translate into effective leadership. The skills of being a good listener, respecting others, being approachable and empathetic should be retained, but there are real and necessary differences in roles and responsibilities.

Trying to be a buddy might make sense to the new leader, but it is confusing to everyone else. It is just no longer true to say, "I'm still just one of the guys," when you sign the paycheck, hold others accountable, and have the ability to fire someone. Everyone else knows this.

Typically, the *buddy* will never hold people accountable (never step into leadership.) Or, after their first one or two uncomfortable occasions of needing to hold others to account, they will give up on friendliness or reasonableness altogether and just harden off. Neither approach is conducive to an enjoyable and effective workplace.

It is far more important to earn the respect of those you lead as opposed to earning the *like*. Sometimes, you will have to choose between the two. Always err toward actions that earn the respect—not like—of your people. Most people would rather a highly competent, respected leader who brings everyone to a high level of performance and workplace harmony than a good buddy who muddles and dithers on tough decisions.

Solution

Learn about emotional intelligence[2] or resonant leadership.[3] In short: the abilities to connect with, understand, and value other people while leading. Accept the very real differences in your role. Having more power or ability than others is a fact of life. Some have more. Some have less. Denying it helps no one. Using it well while treating others with respect and value is of great help.

Approach #3: Toilet Bowl Cleaners

Some new leaders make the mistake of wanting to stay in the trenches. I have often heard leaders (especially entrepreneurial leaders) say, "I'm not afraid to roll up my sleeves and clean out the toilet bowls." And, they often mean it. They might not be referring to an actual toilet bowl. They might be referring to other roles or responsibilities in the company that could be given away. The willingness and attitude may be great. But, if a leader is doing this often, it is nearly always an indicator of a problem.

Sometimes, this is a misplaced perception of equity. Sometimes, they want to deemphasize the difference between their role and others. Sometimes, it is a trust or control issue, "No one does this as well as me." Sometimes, it is an inability to let go of the enjoyable or comfortable work.

Great leaders are willing to do whatever it takes to ensure the success of the organization. They stay in touch with the front lines. They are not *too important*. But, in nearly all cases, it is poor use of a leader's time to clean proverbial toilet bowls.

As a leader, as someone with your unique background and experience, there are some things that only you can do to help serve the organization. You are in a position to create a workplace that has more of a future, that is healthier, and can offer more possibilities to others than before.

Most anyone can figure out and manage the authority to clean a toilet. Very few people in your organization have the ability to generate rapid

---

[2] Birshan, M., T. Meakin, and K. Strovink. 2018. "How New CEOs can Boost Their Odds of Success." *McKinsey Quarterly*. (accessed August 8, 2018).

[3] https://hbr.org/2012/04/the-resonant-team-leader

growth, to secure the future, to save jobs, and to create new opportunities and career paths.

I've watched whole businesses transform themselves within a handful of months when a CEO or owner finally sees this. This transformation not only benefits the company, it benefits everyone in the company. In other words, sometimes it is a disservice to clean the toilet bowl. Doing *whatever it takes* might mean being willing to step away from those kinds of tasks.

I often ask clients, "If you are the only one able to land a multimillion-dollar project/acquire a new business/launch a new service, why are you spending time on something you can pay someone $10 an hour to do? Or even $100 an hour?"

Solution

Do not be pennywise and pound foolish with your money or in your leadership. Learn to see how your choices uniquely create or block opportunities for others. It is far better to build a company that creates jobs or pays for a janitorial service than a company who tries to save pennies by doing it in-house.

Approach #4: The Watchful Enigma

Some new leaders hold back. They watch. They listen. They observe.

And, no one knows they are thinking. For a very long time.

They will frequently tell me, "I'm new here. I'm still trying to learn how things work." I will ask how long they've been in the position. "Oh, I've only been here about year."

A leader may not feel like *The Enigma*. Instead, she might feel busy and overwhelmed with all the work. He might feel like he cannot give confident answers when he still does not know everything. She might feel like, "They've all been here longer than me."

But, everyone else is trying to figure out where you are leading, what your expectations are, and decisions that can be acted on.

It is good to be a learner and to be open. But, if you are engaged in genuine leadership, you will often feel some element of, "I'm not quite sure what the answer is here."

Leaders lead into that. Good leaders know how to lead into the unknown and consistently get people through to the other side. Great leaders define the unknown and help people grow as a result of having gone through it.

Solution

The organization you lead needs leadership now. Not eventually.

Build the leadership ability to *create or clarify vision*. That is the ability to look into the unknown, see or sense what might be on the other side, and describe it so that others are able and willing to follow you there.

View leadership as an essay, not a math problem. You can correct and adjust on the go. Become comfortable making decisions when you do not have all the information. It is often of greater value to make a reasonable decision fast than the right decision slowly. The reason for this is that there are very few *right* decisions out there, in the context of leadership. However, there is a whole range of *better* or *worse* decisions. Nearly all of which can be adjusted if you respond quickly.

Starting Well

If you recognize any of these tendencies in yourself, do not worry about it. These are very common mistakes in new leadership positions. Just correct them.

CHAPTER 11

Without Vision, There Is No Leadership

You can't build what you can't see.

What Your Value, Vision, and Focus Statement Should Accomplish (But Probably Does Not)

It is satisfying, and rare, to hear someone communicate a feeling or thought you have never been able to put into words.

Many of the best leaders do this naturally.

Both the manner and substance of what they say causes other people to say, "Yes! That's what I've been thinking all along!"

Unfortunately, many leaders do not articulate *what* is important. Or *why*. Or *what to do about it.*

This does not mean that they are not good leaders or the right leaders.

It just means that leadership will be more difficult for them. Success will always be more challenging.

The Real Role of Values, Vision, and Focus

In most organizations, reading the value, vision, and focus statement feels like reading the back of a diner menu.

It is what you do when you do not know what else to do. And then, you immediately forget what you have read. Because it does not mean anything, and you have read it a million times anyway:

"We value good sounding words. Not bad ones. And we're-awesome. We do awesome stuff."

I ask owners, executive teams, and board members all the time: What is *most* important to you? What are your values? What is your vision? What is all the effort supposed to add up to? What is your *why?*

Many leaders have sat through some kind of exercise designed to clarify their values and vision. But, few can tell me what they are. Often, their first response is to try to remember where they filed the answers to those questions.

Why? Because what they came up with did not matter. It did not really mean anything to them. It did not reflect what was in their hearts, their sense of driving passion, or purpose.

But, something does matter to them. Something does drive them. But, what is it? As the leader, you need to know what drives you and your organization. It needs to be on the tip of your tongue.

I do not care if you have a slick elevator speech or you need some time to get the thoughts out. The point is: *Do you know where you are going, why you must get there and can you tell anyone?*

The purpose of value, vision, and focus statements is not to sound pretty. It is not for marketing or public relations. Those are side uses.

Here is the purpose: To keep you focused on what really matters.

That is it.

What About "Mission Statements?" What About Our "Why?"

Leaders often get confused (by consultants) around the purpose and use of the words: Values, vision, mission, focus, your *why*, and so on. Some consultants get pretty dogmatic about what each of these words mean and how they relate to each other. But too often, whatever it was they taught does not line up with whatever it is the next consultant says. I *am* sorry about that.

Here is what is important to know: all of these exercises or terms are about creating clarity. They are all designed to create clarity around, "What is important to us, and what are we trying to accomplish?" That clarity should primarily be internal. It should make sense and mean the same thing to everyone who is a part of your organization.

It should be a practical and heavily used tool for setting direction, shaping strategy, setting priorities, architecting culture, creating policies, and so on. Some organizations or consultants get pedantic about verbiage. It does not matter what verbiage you use, as long as you knows what you mean, and it answers the questions, "What is important to us, and what are we trying to accomplish?"

However, so that you know what I mean, I will use and explore the following terms *values*, *vision*, and *focus*.

It's worth spending a little time on this. I've found that most leaders are familiar with the terms but don't really understand their practical use.

Values

Everyone acts based on their values. Everyone makes choices in alignment with their values. This happens naturally. Most people don't even think about it.

In a workplace, if someone is forced to act contrary to their values for very long, they will either leave, find a way to rationalize their compromise, or become mentally ill.[1]

Being in alignment with your values is that powerful.

The challenge is that if you have a group of people, as all organizations do, there is a multitude of values. So, it gets confusing. There is confusion or disagreement over whose values are most important.

Additionally, for any list of values, some will be more highly *valued* than others. For example, in a toss-up between loyalty to family and truthfulness—some people will feel that being loyal to your family is inviolate. Others will feel that being truthful is. The longer your list of values are, the higher the likelihood that some of the stated values strongly guide decisions and behavior, while others seemingly never do.

Effective leadership highlights the few core values that are most meaningful and guiding for their organization. Ones that reflect the values of the group. Ones that everyone can or should rally around, uphold, and

---

[1] Cooper, J. 2019. "Cognitive Dissonance: Where We've Been and Where We're Going." *International Review of Social Psychology* 32, no. 1, 7. DOI: http://doi.org/10.5334/irsp.277

support. The kinds of values that, if they were lacking, would leave you with an entirely different organization altogether.

I find it best to have relatively short and focused value statements. Usually, no more than three to five core values. Most of my clients hate having to pare their lists down and would prefer to have 12 of 20 most important values.

But the reality is these large lists never work. They only create confusion. Ultimately, only a few of the values will regularly be referenced and used as guiding lights. In my opinion, it is important to have an agreement around those few.

Value narratives: Most values are best expressed individual words or short phrases. But even after they are written down, sometimes it isn't clear what is meant.

For example *Family* appears fairly often on value statements for smaller or family owned companies. There are many ways to interpret or apply "Family." I recommend writing a sentence or two to describe what these values mean to you.

One client framed it this way:

Family. We create a safe and welcoming environment for customers and employees. We encourage diversity in ideas, opinions and points of view. (Key Words/Concepts: Belonging, Loyalty, Protect each other, Valuing).

Their definition of "family" is very unique to them and not how others may define it. It is also very guiding when it comes to decision making.

How value statements are used: During the COVID-19 crisis, I was coaching a new executive within a client company. She was struggling with a difficult staffing decision. I suggested that we look at the organizational values for guidance.

At first she resisted saying, "Those things are useless for this kind of situation." Normally, she might be right. But in this case, before she was hired, I had walked the entire ownership and management team through a process of carefully defining their values. We developed them to be specifically to be useful in unforeseen scenarios like this one.

We were talking over the phone. I waited while she pulled out the values and read through them. There was a minute of silence and then, "Oh, I know what to do now. That makes it clear!"

Use your values: Every decision should pass through the filter of your values. Simply ask these questions:

- Does this decision help manifest or demonstrate our values?
- At a minimum, does this decision not contradict our values?

Now, this happens on a personal level all the time. People subconsciously ask themselves, "Is this choice important or right?" We know, intuitively, if we are acting in or out of alignment with what we believe. We may not always act in alignment with our values, but something inside of us lets us know when we have gone off.

This is less common on an organizational level unless you've clearly defined your values and how they shape decisions and behaviors. These are the building blocks of your culture.

When we do this organizationally, something magical happens:

Leadership decisions begin to make sense: There is an internal logic to decisions and policies and practices that everyone understands.

Management becomes easier: People find it easier to know what is expected and what to do and how to act. As a result, they are more likely to self-manage.

Employees are more engaged: because they can see the connection between the values and their responsibilities. When I talk to employees of clients who have gone through a culture change process that emphasized alignment to values, they will regularly reference these values as being part of why they love their job. It matters to people.

Additionally, *the organization is healthier* because people will naturally react to correct dissonance. Dissonance being any kind of decision or behavior or policy that violates the values. A strong culture based around common values is very similar to having a robust immune system organizationally. For example, if an organization truly values *integrity* or *superb customer service* and someone begins to make a decision that is in violation of those values, there will often be a healthy level of pushback until things are in alignment. (Incidentally, these same reinforcing forces are at work in unhealthy cultures driven by unhealthy values.)

Vision

Your vision should be an expression of two things:

1. Your big dreams and aspirations.
2. Your values when fully manifested or expressed in your company.

Early in my career, when I going through a selection process to work in disaster relief, we were brought through a set of team training exercises. My team was taken through an exercise of needing to pitch a tent. The challenge: there were no instructions, none of us had seen the tent before, and everyone except the team leader (myself) was blindfolded. I was not allowed to touch anything or anyone. I could only talk to the team and verbally guide them through assembling the tent. Additionally, we were a multinational team. Not everyone spoke English as a first language and for those of us who did, we were from different continents.

It was hard. Our team spent a lot of time blindly tripping over the pieces of the tent and each other. It was frustrating.

The intended lesson of the exercise was about communication and team dynamics. But, the lesson I took away was *vision matters*.

It is hard to build what you cannot see. Leaders often cannot see the whole picture they are leading toward. But, the more they can see, the clearer their vision is, the more significant is their advantage.

But, it is not enough for the leader to have clear vision. If the team cannot see, success is unlikely. It is hard to lead people who cannot envision what you want them to accomplish. They become dependent on the leader to provide every point of direction. They cannot use their creativity or knowledge because they do not have a vision. Most will stop moving. They will stay in whatever space feels safe, waiting for very specific direction. A few will try to show initiative, but will wander in unhelpful directions.

Organizational vision is not just helpful. It is necessary.

Just the simple act of taking off their blindfolds allows everything to become so much easier.

A leader's ability to articulate the future you are building helps everyone move ahead. Your ability to have a vision for the organization, a department, a team, or an individual is immediately empowering.

The clearer everyone's vision is, the less dependent everyone is on being told what to do. People can begin to figure it out for themselves.

It is a critical and necessary task of leadership to *see and to help others see*. Specifically, to see the same thing: the organizational vision. To not just see that, but to see potential, a future, envision solutions, envision growth, and possibilities.

It is a mark of leadership to be able to inspire a sense of shared vision.

Using Vision Components to write a vision statement: An organizational vision is what you are trying to create or build. It should be highly ambitious but within the realm of what is possible. Even if you don't know how to get there.

Many leaders struggle with coming up with a vision statement. I often recommend using the concept of Vision Components.

For example, if I say the words: "Chocolate chips, flour, eggs, baking soda. Sugar." What do you envision? If you are like most people in my workshops, you probably thought, "Chocolate chip cookies." Even if you didn't, it is highly unlikely you thought, "Pizza!" Instead, you were likely thinking of some kind of similar dessert to a cookie.

Maybe your team isn't in an articulate mood. Or maybe the vision feels kind of there, but not entirely there. Often, for companies going through challenging times, it's hard to look out for years when next month has a big question mark on it.

I recommend defining your Vision Components, your key ingredients to the vision. You can sort out later whether these will be chocolate chip cookies or bars. Whether it should be gooey or crispy. Those differences are a matter of preferences. Not an entire new trip to the store.

So an architectural firm might create something that looks like: *Innovative and interesting projects. Profitable. Secure careers for owners and employees. Fun. Inventing.*

I would translate that into, "We want to build a company that is **sustainably profitable** and provides a **secure future** for the owners and employees. We want to build a culture that is **fun** to work in, that encourages **inventing** and creativity and allows us to work on **innovative and interesting projects.**"

This vision provides direction. It should reflect your values. It guides and simplifies decision making.

It's not a crystal-clear vision. But it is clear enough to start planning and building towards. As you get closer, you'll see more clearly, and can sharpen it as you like.

Focus

The focus is whatever your organization needs to accomplish next to make the vision a reality. It should also reflect your values.

It should be practical and achievable. It should provide priorities and direction for strategy. It should tell you what you should pursue and what you should not pursue.

I have found that, for most organizations, it is difficult to have a very long-range focus. Change is too frequent and rapid. Instead, shorter-range focus periods seem to be more helpful. These are often in the 9- to 18-month time range. But, pick whatever range makes the most sense to you.

Many focus statements sound very simple: "Build and unify the management team." "Improve customer service." "Stabilize cash flow."

They are the next major thing that needs to be accomplished to move toward the vision. It does not mean that other things are not worked on, but it does clarify the priority of where everything sits.

Most organizations understand having a focus. It might be the most tangible piece of the values, vision, and focus pie. A focus lets you know *what our work is* right now.

For the architectural firm I mentioned above, perhaps they've experienced rapid growth. They have doubled each year for the last two years and are struggling to keep up with all of the new work. But with success, they have discovered bottlenecks (and stress) in their management capacity.

They might create a focus for the year of: **Comfortably manage $50mm in projects.**

It keeps you focused. It helps you stay the course or get back on course if you wander. For example, they might choose to be more selective about their work and not grow beyond $50mm this year. By being more selective, they can live into their vision of choosing the most innovative and creative projects.

You should regularly check in on progress toward your focus and update it as needed.

Keep your focus shorter range and actionable.

Your Task as a Leader

Application: Values, Vision, Focus, and Alignment

There should be a direct, logical flow from your values, to the vision you'd like to build, to what you are focusing on right now. When you do this, and you check in on it regularly (remember my comments about strategic review in the last chapter?) you set yourself up to quickly move toward high performance. I've also found that clearly aligned organizations tend to have less unhelpful conflict.

I recently spoke with a partner in a company. She mentioned that, as partners, they tended to not communicate their vision or focus to their employees.

As a result, she said, the employees created their own interpretation of the owners' vision and focus. In this case, that was not a favorable interpretation. It also was not accurate.

What the employees thought was actually demotivating. But, the owners did not communicate to them. So, how could they know differently?

Many leaders love having conversations about values, vision, and focus. But too often they are satisfied with stopping with the high-level conversation. They do not always like having to talk about how these get applied in business decisions in real life.

Decisions like:

- Which contracts that are pursued (or not)
- How hiring practices should be shaped
- How to best make decisions during financially hard times
- Ethical dilemmas
- Improving performance, impact, or profitability

This is precisely why you identify your values, vision, and focus. To create a common formula that will guide all those decisions. This is what supports an aligned organization. A focused organization. An organization with a strong and vibrant culture. Your task as a leader is to make sure that happens.

How to Inspire a Shared Vision

When I was young, I lived on a farm. We raised chickens. It is hard to herd chickens.

You really cannot. If you try, they just scatter. Instead, you give them a common focus (usually food), and they will all come to you.

It is a simple and reliable solution.

As a leader, you do not want to herd chickens. You are not in the chicken herding business. So, why does it sometimes feel like that is what you are doing? Because those you lead do not have a common focus. They do not share the same vision.

What is a Shared Vision and Why Does It Matter?

It's not enough to have a vision. It must be shared.

An inspirational vision is the one that taps into people's intrinsic motivation. Usually, a desire to gain (or not lose) a greater sense of security, significance, or satisfaction. Whatever the vision is, if people see and believe that getting there helps them increase or protect these core motivations, they will pursue it.

When everyone has the same vision, the same mental picture of the future magical things happens:

- You tap into motivation. This increases commitment and performance.
- Alignment is easier. This also increases performance and decreases conflict.
- Management is easier. Everyone knows where to end up. They can use their own problem-solving abilities, as opposed to waiting to be told what to do.

I worked with a partner in a company who had a great vision and great ideas. But, they were not shared by his other partners. He was enormously frustrated by this.

His partners were also frustrated. They felt like they were being accused of failing a vision that they never saw or committed to.

His vision was clear. It was needed. But, vision alone is not enough. It has to be shared.

This leader needed to learn how to talk with his partners. He also would benefit from listening to them and understanding what their vision (or vision components) were. This make it dramatically easier to develop a *shared* vision.

Self-Leadership—Personal Vision

The ability to inspire a shared vision is a critical leadership ability. The only way to lead effectively is to be able to do this.

For some people, developing a personal sense of vision happens naturally. They always have ideas. They cannot help it. For them, the challenge is how to *inspire* and to create a *shared* vision.

For others, a personal sense of vision does not happen as easily. To a limited degree, this is influenced by personality. But, there are visionary people of any kind of personality.

Primarily, the ability to *see* a desirable future has a lot to do with an individual's sense of self-confidence or self-efficacy.

We tend to *dream* to our level of self-efficacy. Whether accurate or not, if I believe I can do things, I will envision myself doing them. If I do not believe I can do things, I tend to not think about them. As a result, a leader needs to become excellent at developing his or her own ability to lead. Here are three tips.

1. Keep the Promises You Make to Yourself

Self-confidence is built through building self-efficacy. Ed Mylett, a business thinker from the financial world, often says that we build our self-confidence by keeping the promises we make to ourselves.

This is as simple as getting up and going to the gym. Not eating the extra donut. Getting the project done today instead of later. Having that conversation that you need to have.

The more consistently you keep the small promises, the easier it is to make and keep the larger ones. The more consistent you are in keeping your promises, the more confident you become in yourself. Self-confidence.

As you make and keep larger and larger promises to yourself, the larger you will naturally dream or envision.

2. Practicing Gratitude and Appreciation

Fear and anger are the two primary inhibitors of successful leadership. Both fear and anger are secondary emotions propelled by something else underneath.

But, you can displace both by practicing gratitude. It is impossible to stay afraid or angry when you are thinking about what you are grateful for.

When you practice appreciation, you are identifying good things in others or in the environment around you. This may often be something or wonderful, or just nice, that does not directly benefit you. But, you are able to appreciate that it exists. For example, someone else's musical skill, or success on a project, or how a colleague handled a difficult situation.

As you learn to appreciate, you teach yourself to see what is *good*. As Zig Ziglar used to say, "Anyone can be a fault finder. I want to be a good finder."

The more you can see good and be grateful for the good that you experience, the easier it is for you to imagine future good for yourself and others. Future good = a potentially inspiring vision.

These habits will shape your perspective, and you will more naturally be able to inspire a shared sense of vision.

3. Helping Others *See*—Building on Strengths

Most people focus on what they do not like, or are not happy with, about their job, their hair, their relationships, politics, other drivers, and so on.

As a result, they are reactive.

When leaders focus on what they do not like—frustrations, offenses, things that are preventing them from doing what they want—they are not leading.

They are reacting.

An inspirational leader will nurture, train, reinforce, and encourage an appreciative mindset in others. This leader will help others identify where they have succeeded, accomplished, won, brought value, or did something well.

This leader will also tell stories (and find the stories) of success from those they lead.

This does two things:

- It helps others build their sense of self-confidence and self-efficacy. It reminds them that they have succeeded, they have overcome challenges, and they have solved problems in the past. They can do so in the future.
- It displaces the fear and anger that can become a *default setting* for many people.

A leader who wants to inspire a shared vision begins by appreciating and helping other recognize past shared successes.

Methods of Developing Vision

There are two basic methods of developing a shared vision. Both have pros and cons. Both tend to work better together.

- **Vision casting:** Vision casting is the classic method that most people think about when they think of inspirational leaders. Effective vision casting happens when a credible leader has a vision for the future that taps into the shared aspirations of others. It is a great idea, which when communicated, other people say, "Yes; I want that!"

- º Pros: It is faster. It is great for emergencies or urgent situations. It is critical when the leader or leadership team functionally retains the real power in a situation (for example, the owner of a private company).
- º Cons: It is often harder to get ownership. People tend to say, "Yes; I want that! You go ahead and do that for us!" Due to lack of ownership, these visions are often less sustainable in the long term.

- **Vision gathering:** Vision gathering is a process of listening to the shared interests, aspirations, and concerns of others. Then working with them to develop a picture of the future that meets those shared interests, aspirations, and concerns. It is usually the best approach when leadership has limited power and in situations where there is a need for long-term commitment.

  - º Pros: Vision gathering tends to stick. The process created is buy-in and ownership. It does not require that any particular leader have the vision, so anyone can pursue. It is what I do when I help clients develop their vision. I gather it from them and help bring it into focus.
  - º Cons: It takes more time upfront. It is less predictable or controllable. It requires a high level of skill to guide a group of people through difficult conversation to consensus without creating a flavorless, meaningless *vision by committee*, which is what almost everyone does.

The best answer is usually a combination of the two. Leaders need to be careful to listen to the group. The group often needs a leader to help them think even larger and get unstuck from endless dithering.

The Formula for a Shared Vision: Credibility, Shared Aspirations, and Ownership

To effectively inspire a shared vision and lead it to reality, you need three ingredients:

- Credibility: There needs to be trust for the leader, each other, and the process.
- Shared aspirations: The vision needs to embrace the shared interests of the group.
- Ownership: The group needs to feel a sense of commitment and responsibility to ensure the vision comes to life.

When a shared vision is lacking, it is often because it is missing one of these ingredients.

- Credibility + Shared aspirations–Ownership = Unsustainability. The effort will run out of gas.
- Shared aspirations + Ownership–Credibility = Fence sitting. People hedge their bets, create factions, or constantly negotiate their engagement
- Ownership + Credibility–Shared aspirations = Turf battles. Without a shared focus, people develop and protect what is individually important.

Those being led need to believe that their aspirations will be met through pursuing this vision. Everyone needs to own and be committed to seeing it through.

Would you like free tools to help you build a shared vision? Go to www.christianmuntean.com/resources/

CHAPTER 12

How to Excel in the Everyday Tasks of Leadership

Effective leadership is not about making speeches or being liked; leadership is defined by results not attributes.

— Peter Drucker

Why Great Delegators Make Great Leaders

At the party of leadership skills, Delegation is the drably dressed, quiet guy sitting in the corner. Seems boring.

People talk to him when they have to. Just enough to be polite. And, because he is sitting next to the chips. Then off to find someone else more interesting.

However, on their way home, they receive this text: "OMG! OMG! OMG! That nerd guy! He's a gazillionaire! He makes rockets or creates genes or buys and sells countries or something!"

It turns out that Delegation only seems boring.

Actually, it turns out that Delegation is just Super Successful Leadership's alter ego. His street disguise.

Delegation is what Super Successful Leadership looks like when he puts on glasses and covers up his tights.

Leaders Delegate: Great Leaders Are Great Delegators

Leadership is about a lot of things.

One of those indispensable things is the ability to help other people accomplish a lot. That is delegation.

In fact, if someone cannot give away vision, goals, tasks, responsibilities, authority, decisions, and resources to other people so more can be accomplished, they cannot lead. They do not have the basic ability to lead.

Even if they look good in a suit. And, are fun to talk to. And, have a fancy title.

There is a direct correlation with someone's ability to effectively lead more (more people, bigger budgets, greater complexity, numbers of projects, etc.) and their ability to delegate.

That works the other way too. Leaders who struggle with just trying to keep up with today's crisis (forget about trying to build or sustain a vision) are also poor at delegating.

Time Struggles Suggest Delegation Struggles

It is common for my executive and leadership coaching clients to feel busy, stretched, and overwhelmed.

Too busy to learn to be less busy.

It is a catch-22. Of their own making.

Time management is just another way of saying priority management.

Great leaders place a priority on discovering ways to give away work. To give away responsibility. They are great at helping other people do.

The degree to which your priority is helping others be successful at doing things as opposed to you doing things is the degree to which you are actually leading.

This is a primary role and responsibility for a leader. The artful mastery of the skill of delegation.

The more influence, people, and resources someone leads, the better they need to rely on the skill of delegating to be successful.

Leaders who do not or will not delegate limit the growth of others. They limit the growth of their teams or organizations. They limit the overall growth to their individual capacity as opposed to the collective capacity.

Delegation Requires a Mindset Shift

Leaders who get the best out of a team think in terms of leverage, building trust, accepting imperfection, and serving others by preparing for them to succeed.

To make up a statistic: At least 80 percent of a leader's time should be spent on activities such as:

- Vision-building
- Creating focus
- Identifying and working on priorities
- Gathering and distributing resources
- Coaching, mentoring, encouraging, and appreciating
- Challenging and generating accountability

Perhaps, as much as 20 percent of their time might be spent on *doing*.

The reality is that many people in positions of leadership spend most of their time *doing*. Not leading.

They still *do* engineering, or see patients, or take cases, or make sales, or build things or fix things.

They get stressed at the idea of actually doing the work of leadership. They believe they need to hold onto the doing and add leading on top of it.

But, that is not it.

Delegation (aka leadership) is largely about letting go.

To grow, to be successful, to expand, to lead—you have to know how to let go.

How to Prepare to Delegate Naturally, Easily, and Effectively

I used to work in construction. I grew up around contractors and know many contractors.

Contractors, whose businesses stay small, will often do the work themselves and hire someone to be a *gofer*. You know, "Go fer this hammer,"

"Go fer that board." That is a small form of delegation that never rises above assigning tasks.

They usually do not know what work needs to be done until the day of. Or minute of.

So, they have small companies. Usually very few employees.

Contractors who build larger businesses will never do the work themselves. Instead, they hire foremen or subcontractors who hire their own workers. The large contractors provide the plans. They tell them the outcomes to work to and let them do it.

They are larger because they delegate.

To delegate, they have to know what they want far in advance of starting the project. When they make a change, they plan and communicate the change. They have as many jobs going on as they can win and as many employees as they can successfully delegate to.

To grow your skills in delegation, here is what you need to do.

Adjust Priorities

As aforementioned, you need to shift your priorities from getting stuff done to empowering individuals and teams to get stuff done. Without this priority shift, you will always work against yourself.

Adjust How You Spend Your Time

This is easier once you adjust your priorities. Make sure your calendar reflects your new priorities. You should have regular periods of time preblocked in your calendar that you set aside for planning, communicating, coaching, and creating accountability.

You cannot lead or delegate well by squeezing the work of leadership or delegation into whatever leftover time you have.

Creating the Same Sheet of Music

Learn to plan for the purpose of communicating.

Planning is valuable for many reasons. However, one of the key reasons is that many leaders are too in their heads and assume everyone knows what they want, or they have not taken the time to figure out what they want and are figuring it out as they go.

Either way, it leaves everyone standing around, waiting for you. Get the plans out of your head and someplace where others can see them. It is like taking the time to develop blueprints. Then you and everyone else can figure out how they fit into the plan, what they can carry responsibility for, what resources are needed, and so on.

If you do not know the plans, take time to figure them out.

I know this is tough for some leaders. But, it is an important discipline if you want growth and if you truly want to empower others.

This is often why having planning sessions with your team or working with a coach or consultant can be very helpful—to draw out the plans.

Either way, the more everyone has a shared sense of the value, vision and focus and a clear sense of the part they play in getting it done, the easier it will be to delegate.

How to Use Planning

Any planning process should automatically lead into delegation. Any good planning process should result in:

- Describing the key goals
- Clarifying team or individual roles and responsibilities as they relate to the plan
- Understanding the resources needed for success and when they are needed
- Establishing time frames: when projects need to be started and completed
- Identify the indicators of success

What Individuals Need to Be Successfully Delegated To

People need three things to be successful when you delegate to them:

- **Clear expectations:** They need clarity on what is wanted, by when, and what success looks like. This is where planning is so helpful for you and them.

- **Sufficient skills:** They need to have the basic skills to be successful.
- **Authority or resources:** They need to have enough decision-making authority and access to resources to be successful. You can forecast this easier with good planning.

If your attempts to delegate are not working, it is probably due to a deficiency in one of these three areas:

- Clear expectations + Authority or resources–Sufficient skills = *Ineffective effort*
- Clear expectations + Skills–authority–Authority or resources = *Frustrated effort*
- Authority or resources + Skills–clear–Clear expectations = *Misdirected effort*

It is up to you, the leader, to ensure that your people and teams are given and are operating from clear expectations, sufficient skills, and supplied with enough authority and resources to be successful. Your work is to focus on those things. Let them follow through on implementation.

Over time, as expectations become clearer and clearer—as skills grow, as you learn to delegate authority and resources—you will find that it is also easier for your team to lead and delegate to others, which just expands how much your organization can accomplish.

The Importance of Good Meetings

According to the personality tests out there, I have clear introverted tendencies. A good day for me is a day with a lot of alone time. I think I am pretty good company. For just me.

In spite of this, I like meetings. In fact, I love them.

The reason I love meetings is because I:

- Have a *purpose* for the meetings I go to
- Have (or look for) opportunities to *give value* at meetings
- *Get value* out of the meetings I go to

My assumption is that for the readers of this book, most can choose the meetings they attend. In fact, you may be the primary initiator of meetings. So, I am assuming that you have the ability to influence how meetings are run.

If there is no purpose or value in a meeting, I will not go. Or, I try to change how it is run and bring back purpose and value. I usually do this by asking questions to flesh out some level of purpose or value. This is usually successful, and if done with the right attitude, is well-received.

If I am unable to bring value to a meeting and get value out of a meeting, I will stop attending. Why be there?

People know when they are at time wasting meetings. Many people feel they need to attend these meetings, or actually are required to attend. They hate being at time wasting meetings.

Fixing your meetings is very easy way to dramatically increase your leadership impact.

A Secret about Meetings

One of the most heavily used tools in my tool bag is that of a meeting facilitator. I often help plan, organize, and facilitate meetings of all kinds. Many years ago, when I first started, I bought a lot of books on *how to* facilitate a good meeting.

Many of the books talk about things like icebreakers, exercises, games you can play, and so on. But, here is what I learned.

The only people who want those kinds of things in their meetings are the people who are:

- Forced to go to a meeting but do not understand why they are there (or do not care)
- Are not sure how they will give or receive value from the meeting

What I found is that people want to be productive, feel like their time is being used well, and are engaged in the conversation. They like this better than icebreakers, stage shows, and trust falls. Everyone hates trust falls.

One Secret to Instantly Improve All Your Meetings

Only have meetings about things that matter and with the people they matter to.

But *what if that is not enough?* As it turns out, having meetings about important things with the right people still does not ensure meeting success. Lots of those meetings are miserable too. Sit through a meeting at your local assembly or a community planning committee sometime, and you will see what I am talking about.

The problem is that many meetings just are not facilitated or led well.

The POP Principle to Make Every Meeting an Awesome Meeting

Only three things are needed to run awesome meetings. Purpose. Outcome. Process. POP. If your meeting is not awesome, it is because one or more of these is off.

Purpose

Every meaning should have a clear purpose. Whether it is a team accountability check-in to make sure everyone is on track, an ad-hoc meeting to plan a birthday party or an executive meeting to address a risk management issue—your meeting should have a purpose.

You should never have a regular *Monday Manager's Meeting* where no one has anything to talk about and/or nothing needs to be discussed. Never default to agendas comprised of reports that no one listens to and announcements that could be communicated through a memo or e-mail.

Application

Answer these questions, "How does this meeting serve the larger purpose of answering our 'Why'?" "How does this meeting help us take tangible steps toward fulfilling our values, living out our vision, and accomplishing our focus or focus?"

If your answers are not compelling, then the meeting should either find its purpose or should not exist. Anything else is time wasting.

Outcome

Every meeting should answer a question. Every meeting should produce a result. Most meetings cannot handle a lot of questions or produce a lot of results. So, there should be at least one clear question and one desired result.

This could look like: "Is everyone on track to be successful today?" to "How should our company respond to this changing technology?" to "What should our compensation philosophy be?" When those questions engage the right people, you have a productive meeting.

You should walk into the meeting with one result or outcome the meeting needs to produce. If you accomplish that result, and it makes sense, go on to the next one.

Meetings that are about dozens of things are usually meetings that accomplish very little. Do not confuse a packed agenda with a productive one.

Application

Answer these questions, "What does this meeting need to accomplish?" "How will we know it was accomplished?"

Process

Different meetings require different processes. It hurts me on the inside when I watch someone pull a small group together for an informal meeting and then use Robert's Rules of Order.

Robert's Rules of Order or any other form of parliamentary procedure is designed to manage the discussion of a large group of people who may not work together well and tend to get off-track. It is a highly controlled process designed to mitigate or guide conflict and move toward decisions. It has a role.

It does not work well for exploring ideas, engaging broad input, or connecting with a wide audience.

Designing and leading an effective *process* is a skill, a science, and an art. More than what I can do justice to here.

If you struggle with creating an effective process, here are four resources (I get nothing from this) that can help you improve your meeting processes.

No Fail Meetings by Michael Hyatt
Death by Meeting by Patrick Lencioni
Harvard Business Review Guide to Making Every Meeting Matter
Facilitating with Ease! by Ingrid Bens (for more advanced skill development)

For important or complicated meetings, it frequently makes the most sense to bring in someone skilled in the ability to facilitate.

Application

What process will best serve the purpose and produce the outcomes needed at your meeting? If you do not know, who can you ask?

The purpose of the POP approach is to make sure your meetings produce results.

Why go through all the effort and cost to bring people together if you are not going to achieve a meaningful result?

Never have meetings that are not producing results. Cut out sections of the meeting or agenda items that do not contribute to results.

The more focused and valuable your meetings are, the more awesome they will be. And, people will tell you so.

The Six Keys for How Successful Leaders Make Decisions

1. Faster Decisions

Successful leaders make decisions more quickly. They realize that leadership is far more like writing an essay than like solving a math problem. There is room for adjustments and correction—but only if you start writing.

When I work with leaders who struggle with *analysis paralysis*, it's usually caused by one of the two things:

- Fear of making a mistake
- Fear of what others will think

Fear will never produce good decisions. I am not a fan of sloppy work, foolish or rash decisions. But, there is more success associated with leaders who were not afraid of making a mess than leaders who were afraid to act.

Having said this, making a good decision quickly is a skill that takes two things:

1. Practice. You get better at it the more you practice. So, make and learn from your decisions quickly.
2. Preparation. Good, quick decisions do not come from a vacuum. They come from preparation. As you practice, you learn how to prepare. Bring the right people, information, and processes to your decision-making.

2. Alignment with Values and Purpose

The clearer you and your team are on your values, vision, and focus, the easier it is to make decisions.

It works like this: A decision-making opportunity comes up, and you ask yourselves:

- Does this decision help express or manifest our values?
- Does this decision help move us toward our vision?
- Does this decision help us achieve our focus?

Is your answer to these questions, "Yes?" Then, it is probably the right decision. At a minimum, your decisions should never violate your values, pull you away from your vision, or distract your focus.

This is why, being clear and having honest and frequent conversations about your values, vision, and focus as a leader and an organization are so important. It helps you and everyone else make better decisions faster.

3. Criteria for Good Decisions

Sometimes, you will have options that are in alignment with your values, vision, and focus, and it might not be obvious which option is the best one.

Having predetermined criteria for decision-making will help you identify and make good decisions more quickly.

An example of decision-making criteria often considers:

- Ease of implementation: How easy should implementation be? What is the maximum acceptable level of difficulty?
- Impact or benefit: What is the minimum acceptable result? What is ideal?
- Cost: What are the budget or cost parameters?
- Financial impacts: return on investment (ROI), impact on cash flow, potential savings, and so on
- Post-decision flexibility (versus being *locked in*): Can we can the decision? Or are we stuck with it?
- Risk: What are our risk tolerances?

These are just examples. If you are choosing someone for a leadership position, you may use a different set of criteria such as:

- Experience: Do we want specific kinds of experience? Length of experience?
- Skills: What specific skills are required? What are preferred?
- Demographics: How should we diversify? Age? Gender? Ethnicity? Language?
- Reputation: Does it matter if they already have a reputation in the field? What reputation and with whom are we looking for?
- Relationships: Who do they know that we want to know?

This is a technique I learned as a mediator. When parties were making difficult decisions and tended to get stuck, I would work with them to define what their interests were in a good decision. In other words, we would define the qualities of a good and mutually acceptable decision in advance. Then, we explored options.

This will help you identify more options than you initially were aware of. It will help you avoid the conflict that can come with decision-making. It will also help you recognize a good decision more quickly. This is a good process if you are making decisions alone but is extremely valuable if you are making decisions with a group.

4. Identify Options: At Least 3, But 20 Is Better

I will often give clients one sticky note a piece and 15 minutes. I will tell them to write down the first 20 ideas that come to them. They do not have to be good, bad, or even possible. Just the ideas that come to mind.

They always look shocked, as if I just asked them to sign up for an ultra-marathon. "Twenty ideas? No one has 20 ideas! I'll use up all my ideas for the rest of my life!"

Then they start to write. They charge through the first handful of ideas. Then they get stuck, ask if they can quit, and start tapping their pens and give me dirty looks.

After they eventually force themselves through the next five to eight ideas, the dam bursts. The remaining ideas just start popping out.

Usually, the idea they end up choosing is the one or a combination of the last few ideas they had.

I do not know why it works like this, but it does. Reliably. And, it takes less than 15 minutes.

But, do this *after* you have gotten clear about your value and purpose and *after* you have developed decision-making criteria. That restriction, interestingly, will help you come up with *more* ideas. And, once you have got a list, the good ideas will be obvious.

There are several purposes to this exercise: one is to break up binary thinking. That there is a *right* and *wrong* answer out there. There seldom is. Another is that it is easier to make better decisions if you have better options to choose from. The first set of ideas that people have are often not their best ideas. Lastly, the best ideas often emerge from combinations of ideas.

5. *The 80 Percent Rule*

For most decisions that need to be made, perfection is not only unlikely, but it is also impossible. Sometimes, there just is not a perfect answer, or approach. I have found that it is enormously freeing for my clients, and they start making real progress toward their goals when I suggest that they only try to get their decisions up to *80 percent right.*

Most of my clients are Type A high achievers, who want to be right in everything. For most of what they pursue being more *right* than 80 percent is often unhelpful and the time and effort it takes to get there does not justify itself.

Eighty percent is still a B. It is honor roll. It is good enough. When you get to 80 percent, make your decision and move on.

6. *A Sense of Peace*

When I was a teenager, a mentor gave me advice. She said, "Don't do anything that causes you to lose your peace."

I will be honest. At that time, I did not know what she meant or how to practice that. But, I tried to listen and understand. What I have discovered is that this is something that takes practice and reflection. So, you might not get it your first time out.

I started paying attention to decisions and choices I made—even small ones. I started to ask the question, "Does doing or deciding this cause me to stay at peace? Or am I feeling disturbed, dissonant, or agitated because of the choice I made?"

I have learned that it is very helpful to stop making choices that cause me to lose my peace.

This does not mean that I do not make hard choices. Even painful choices. Being at peace does not mean things are not sometimes difficult or painful.

Side note: Most people experience a sense of *predecision* anxiety. This has been scientifically identified. Before decisions, many people experience a level of anxiety. Then they make a decision, any decision, to relieve themselves of that anxiety.

That is not the kind of peace that I am talking about. That is a false peace.

What I think my mentor meant was that some decisions keep us in alignment with our values and purpose in life. When we are out of alignment, we feel it. We are dissonant.

We cannot lead well when we are out of alignment with ourselves. Keep your peace.

Three Additional Practices That Help with Making Faster Decisions

1. Habits

Barack Obama became known for having a simple wardrobe. His reason was to cut down on decision-making. He needed to make so many decisions every day, and he did not want his clothes choices to consume any of his bandwidth.

For example, I eat a half-dozen boiled eggs every morning. I never think about what I will have for breakfast. I can eat them while driving my kids to school. And farmers like me.

Create habits around everyday actions so that you do not have to spend your energy and attention on making routine decisions.

2. Mentors and Coaches

The highest performers in the world, in any arena, have mentors and coaches. The people who say, "It's lonely at the top," are people who have isolated themselves.

From your perspective, it might look like they are a high performer. But, they may still paddling in puddles compared to the giants. Additionally, they usually plateau, get weird, or get into trouble. Don't isolate. Surround yourself with people who can mentor and coach you in different areas to continue to grow.

Mentors and coaches challenge your decisions, bring in outside perspective to your decision-making process, and help hold you accountable to the decisions you make.

3. Reflection

Being able to reflect on the results of a decision is an important practice. It is just a process of asking questions:

- Did this accomplish what it intended to achieve?
- How do I feel about the process we went through?
- Do I have peace?
- Is there anything I will change the next time I make that kind of decision?

The Practical Wisdom of Decision-Making

Decision-making is a muscle and a skill. You practice it. Over time, it gets easier. If you follow the recommendations mentioned, you will make better decisions, faster. This is the art of learning the wisdom you need as a leader: Knowing the right decision to make, when and how.

Decide Fast, Act Big

In my first executive role, I had little guidance from the board in terms of where to take the organization or how to get there.

I made big decisions early on that were painful. But ultimately, they were beneficial in terms of improving accountability, decreasing risk, and improving management systems.

I did not realize it until later, but what I was really doing was getting my *arms around* the organization. Making sure I understood it, could guide it, increase its transparency and accountability, and could operate it.

Which is fine. In fact, I made major moves toward best practices. Except for one major problem:

I was slow to make decisions that would produce growth. Growth often requires an investment of some kind. It often requires risk.

In my case, I was afraid of making mistakes. So, I did a great job of getting everything very neat and tidy. We were incredibly hard-working, thrifty, and productive in relation to our size.

But for years, we were limited in growth. Growth only started when I started making big decisions, all of which carried risk. Most of which worked. Some did not.

In the final analysis, though, *not* making big moves was more costly than making big moves. You can recover and learn from a mistake. You might even convert it into something valuable.

You can't do anything with inertia.

How to Stop Playing Whack-a-Mole with Problems

I have often found it interesting that the CEO of a small, simply organized company may be completely harried and distracted. Yet, the CEO of a large, complex operation may be relaxed, focused, and on point most of the time.

It can be very difficult for the first CEO to believe that any other reality is possible. The latter CEO usually knows full well that other realities are possible and works hard to choose and create the one he or she wants.

It is the outside perspective that another reality is possible that can help the first CEO begin to break free. To get out of their tunnel. To stop playing an endless cosmic game of whack-a-mole.

The average executive who I talk to feels stuck, endlessly hammering little moles: meetings, routines, work crises, staff issues, lawsuits, big projects, urgent opportunities...

They do not have the energy for creative thinking or problem-solving. They do not feel they have the time to work preventatively, so they work reactively.

They fall victim to whack-a-mole leadership. Feeling like they are required to stand there, hypervigilant, and whack problems as they occur.

An outside perspective allows you to answer important whack-a-mole questions like:

- Can you actually win a game of whack-a mole?
- What is your purpose in playing the game?
- Who made the rules, and who says you need to follow them?
- Is there any ethical reason to not just unplug the game? Or hold a board over the moles so none can pop up?

The point is leaders fall into a routine informed and shaped by real and imagined responsibilities, needs, and expectations of others.

Why You Need an Outside Perspective

Break up Rutted Thinking

Have you ever started on an errand, and then a couple of turns later, realize you are actually on the route to work?

As leaders, habits can be enormously powerful tools for helping us be more productive and focused.

If they are the right habits.

Sometimes they are not. Or, they were the right habits to get us where we are, but they are not the right habits to get us where we want to be.

An outside perspective can help us get out of ruts that may no longer be serving us well.

Build New Strengths

The body, brain, and relationships are naturally lazy.

In fitness, when we first start a new workout regimen, it is hard and takes a lot of effort. However, if you stay in the same routine, you will end up getting very efficient at that routine.

It no longer takes the same effort to complete the routine. Which is great if you are learning a skill—not great if you are trying to build strength or burn calories.

To build new levels of strength or keep burning calories, we need change. It is the same in our mental growth and our work or any other relationships. We need some kind of new input, nearly always from the outside, that either challenges us to change our pace, change our form or change our workout altogether.

Expose New Opportunities

I have always been impressed at how I can look at a specific situation a thousand times, believe I understand it well, and then meet someone who approaches it completely differently. And more effectively.

New eyes help us see new opportunities. Perhaps in how we work. Perhaps in potential partnerships. Perhaps in innovation.

Identify Potential Challenges

Outside perspectives help us identify and avoid challenges we may not see coming. Our experience may feel special to us, but it is possible others have seen it before. We might have something to learn from them that could save us an expensive or tiring lesson.

How to Get and Maintain an Outside Perspective

1. Read Books and Listen to Podcasts

Especially on topics we do not normally read or from people who think differently than we do.

2. Attend Conferences

Find conferences with speakers who can help you see differently, especially conferences that attract attendees who are excelling in an area you want to grow.

3. Unplugged Vacations

Some people find these easy to take. Most leaders never unplug. Just like athletes need to rest to be able to grow, leaders need to rest to restore creative thinking and visionary perspectives.

4. Leadership Roundtables or Mastermind Groups

These are groups of peers, sometimes in the same industry, sometimes not, who meet regularly to help each other grow. They are usually facilitated and often have access to outside speakers or thought leaders.

5. Outside Advisor

The right advisor, often a paid coach or consultant, will often have a very broad outside perspective and can quickly help you zero in on changes or growth you want to pursue.

6. External Training

Sending someone to be trained in a different environment or context can help introduce new ideas to your organization. Be prepared to explore or engage the new ideas that come back.

7. External Leadership

The most direct way to get an outside perspective is to hire external leadership or bring in external leaders or advisors for your board.

Conclusion

The architects I have known have great imaginations. They see the use of space and structure, not just as walls and rooms, but as methods of communication and influence.

Executive leadership is similar. It is an opportunity to be an architect of your organization's culture and structure. It is a platform from which you can build the people you lead and influence the communities you are involved in.

For some people, the experience of becoming an executive is jarring: Everyone looking to you, needing you to come up with answers, hoping you have right ones.

There is real responsibility and real pressure.

But, it can also be real fun. Lean into building your skills as an *architect* of culture. Learn to see teams and systems as the spaces and structures with which you build.

Most people live lives where their decisions are carefully reduced and controlled. It is a way of avoiding mistakes. Or, if they cannot do that, they avoid being responsible.

You are going to make mistakes. Humility, if you cultivate it, will save you.

You are going to have to make hard and even painful decisions. Empathy, if you do not misplace it, will protect you.

Take responsibility. It is the fastest path to growth.

Build a clear vision and relentlessly pursue it.

Care about your people. Help them do great things.

That is a good way to succeed.

Bibliography

Birshan, M., T. Meakin, K. Strovink. 2018. "HowNnew CEOs Can Boost their Odds of Success" *McKinsey Quarterly.* https://mckinsey.com/featured-insights/leadership/how-new-ceos-can-boost-their-odds-of-success, (accessed August 8, 2018)

Price, H. 2019. "What Is Resonant Leadership?" *Culture Amp Blog* https://cultureamp.com/blog/what-is-resonant-leadership/, (accessed June 25, 2020)

Daniel, G. 2020. "Emotional Intelligence." *Daniel Goleman* http://danielgoleman.info/topics/emotional-intelligence/, (accessed January 7, 2020)

David, C. 2020. "What Is Appreciative Inquiry?" David Cooper Rider and Associates https://davidcooperrider.com/ai-process/, (accessed January 7, 2020)

Duhigg, C. 2016. "What Google Learned from Its Quest to Build the Perfect Team." *The New York Times Magazine.* https://nytimes.com/2016/02/28/magazine/what-google-learned-from-its-quest-to-build-the-perfect-team.html, (accessed January 7, 2020)

Ed Mylett. 2020. "Entrepreneur, Ranked Top 50 Wealthiest Under 50." *Ed Mylett* https://edmylett.com/, (accessed January 7, 2020)

Greenleaf, R.K. 1977. *Servant Leadership: A Journey into the Nature of Legitimate Power and Greatness.*

Jiang, K., J. Hu, Y. Hong, H. Liao, and S. Liu. 2016. "Do it Well and do It Right: The Impact of Service Climate and Ethical Climate on Business Performance and the Boundary Conditions." *Journal of Applied Psychology* 101, no. 11, pp. 1553–1568.

Mindset Scholars Network. 2019. *Growth Mindset, Learning Mindsets.* https://mindsetscholarsnetwork.org/learning-mindsets/growth-mindset/ (accessed April 23, 2019)

Pentland, A. 2012. "The New Science of Building Great Teams." *Harvard Business Review.* https://hbr.org/2012/04/the-new-science-of-building-great-teams. (accessed January 7, 2020)

Peter, L.J., and R. Hull. 1969. *The Peter Principle,* New York City: William Morrow & Company, Inc.

TINYpulse Employee Engagement and Organizational Culture Report. 2014. "The 7 Key Trends Impacting Today's Workplace." *2014 Employee Engagement Organizational Culture Report.* https://tinypulse.com/2014-employee-engagement-organizational-culture-report (accessed January 7, 2020).

Zig Ziglar. 2012. "Zig Ziglar—Be a Good Finder!" *The Happiness Network.* https://youtube.com/watch?v=Ip3OWelIrkE, (accessed January 7, 2020).

About the Author

Christian Muntean works with leaders of fast-growth companies and owners of businesses who are planning for profitable and meaningful exits. He is an executive coach and a trusted advisor to boards and executive teams. His clients range from start-ups to Fortune 500 companies. He has supported many of his clients to become industry leaders and models of success.

He is the author of *Conflict and Leadership* and a writer for many business publications, including regular contributions to Forbes.com. He has an M.A. in Organizational Leadership and is a Certified Exit Planning Advisor.

Christian lives in Anchorage, Alaska with his wife and three children. He enjoys woodworking and practices Brazilian Jiu-Jitsu.

Christian's website address is www.christianmuntean.com and his email is christian@christianmuntean.com

Index

OTHER TITLES IN THE HUMAN RESOURCE MANAGEMENT AND ORGANIZATIONAL BEHAVIOR COLLECTION

- *Leadership In Disruptive Times* by Sattar Bawany
- *Level-Up Leadership* by Michael J. Provitera
- *The Truth About Collaborating* by Dr. Gail Levitt
- *Uses and Risks of Business Chatbots* by Tania Peitzker
- *Lean on Civility* by Tania Peitzker
- *Three Key Success Factors for Transforming Your Business* by Michael Hagemann
- *Hiring for Fit* by Janet Webb
- *Uniquely Great* by Lucy English
- *The Relevance of Humanities to the 21st Century Workplace* by Michael Edmondson
- *Untenable* by Gary Covert
- *Chief Kickboxing Officer* by Alfonso Asensio
- *Cross-Cultural Leadership Studies* by Alan S. Gutterman
- *Comparative Management Studies* by Alan S. Gutterman
- *No Cape Required* by Bob Hughes and Helen Caton Hughes
- *Practicing Management* by Alan S. Gutterman
- *Women Leaders* by Sapna Welsh and Caroline Kersten

We Are The Publisher For Concise and Applied Business Books

The Collection listed above is one of 30 business subject collections that Business Expert Press has grown to make BEP a premiere publisher of print and digital books. Our concise and applied books are for...

- Professionals and Practitioners
- Faculty who adopt our books for courses
- Librarians who know that BEP's Digital Libraries are a unique way to offer students ebooks to download, not restricted with any digital rights management
- Executive Training Course Leaders
- Business Seminar Organizers

Business Expert Press books are for anyone who needs to dig deeper on business ideas, goals, and solutions to everyday problems. Whether one print book, one ebook, or buying a digital library of 110 ebooks, we remain the affordable and smart way to be business smart. For more information, please visit www.businessexpertpress.com, or contact sales@businessexpertpress.com.

Printed in the USA
CPSIA information can be obtained
at www.ICGtesting.com
JSHW011104141123
52031JS00003B/10